100 Clever, Funny, and Insightful Lessons for Life

It's a Dog-Eat-Dog World and Cats Are Waiting Tables

HOWARD BOOKS
A DIVISION OF SIMON & SCHUSTER
New York   London   Toronto   Sydney

Martin Babb
Illustrated by Ron Wheeler

About the Author

Martin Babb is currently the Associate Pastor, Education at Springfield Baptist Church in Springfield, Tennessee. He has also served at Calvary Baptist Church and Pulaski Heights Baptist Church in Little Rock, Arkansas, and has had many articles published in newspapers and magazines. Martin is the author of *When Did Caesar Become a Salad and Jeremiah a Bullfrog?* He lives with his wife, Beverly, and their two children, Meredith and David. They also have two Chihuahuas, Molly and Tiny, and a Yorkshire terrier, Hershey. Martin can be contacted at mkbabb@bellsouth.net.

About the Illustrator

Ron Wheeler has been drawing cartoons full-time professionally since 1980. His call from the Lord is to create cartoons to be a communication vehicle for spreading God's truths. Ron and his wife, Cindy, have been married since 1984, and they homeschool their three children, Audrey, Byron, and Grace. Ron and Cindy both grew up in Nebraska and have lived in Kansas City, Missouri, for over two decades. You can learn more about Ron and how God gave him this calling and see more samples of his work at www.cartoonworks.com.

This book is dedicated to Juanita, Jerry, and Stephen Hatfield, and Gracie Hatfield Hilton, in memory of Lawson Hatfield. He was my first supervisor out of seminary. I loved working with him. He was a unique and wonderful man.

◆

It is also dedicated to Charlie Martin, in memory of his wife, Susie. Susie was a good friend and a pretty good softball player at Calvary Baptist Church in Little Rock. She had a similar sense of humor to mine. I miss her laugh.

I miss both of these individuals, but the pleasant memories live on.

Our purpose at Howard Books is to:
* *Increase faith* in the hearts of growing Christians
* *Inspire holiness* in the lives of believers
* *Instill hope* in the hearts of struggling people everywhere
Because He's coming again!

Published by Howard Books, a division of Simon & Schuster, Inc.
1230 Avenue of the Americas, New York, NY 10020

It's a Dog-Eat-Dog World, and Cats Are Waiting Tables © 2006 by Martin Babb

www.howardpublishing.com

Library of Congress Cataloging-in-Publication Data
Babb, Martin, 1952–
  Its a dog-eat-dog world and cats are waiting tables : 100 clever and insightful lessons for life / by Martin Babb ; Illustrated by Ron Wheeler.
      p. cm.
  ISBN-13: 978-1-58229-582-4 (tradepaper)
  ISBN-10: 1-58229-582-4 (tradepaper)
  1. Christian life—Meditations.   2. Christian life—Anecdotes.   3. Christian life—
Humor.   4. Christian life—Caricatures and cartoons.
  I.   Wheeler, Ron. II. Title.
  BV4501.2.B33   2006
  248.402'07—dc22   2006021601
06 07 08 09 10 11 12 13   10 9 8 7 6 5 4 3 2 1

HOWARD is a registered trademark of Simon & Schuster, Inc.
Manufactured in the United States of America.
For information regarding special discounts for bulk purchases, please contact Simon & Schuster Special Sales at 1-800-456-6798 or business@simonandschuster.com.

Edited by Jennifer Stair
Cover design by Rex Bohn
Photography/illustrations by Ron Wheeler

Contents

CONTENTS

2. You Can't Let Sleeping Dogs Lie if You
Let the Cat out of the Bag
(lessons in life from nonhumans)

3. If Life Is a Bed of Roses, Then Someone
Flipped My Mattress
(lessons from day-to-day living)

Contents

4. *Does History Repeat Itself Because Nobody Listened the First Time?*
(lessons from history about His story)

5. Give Me the Remote Control So I Can
Change My Channel of Blessing
(lessons in sharing the gospel)

Contents

6. *If You Are Early to Bed and Early to Rise,
You'll Probably Miss Your Teenager Coming Home
(lessons from the family)*

CONTENTS

Contents

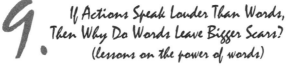

9. If Actions Speak Louder Than Words, Then Why Do Words Leave Bigger Scars?
(lessons on the power of words)

CONTENTS

10. *Joy to the World, the Lord Is Calm
    (lessons from the holidays)*

Contents

Chapter 1:

Tell Me the Story of Jesus, but I Don't Want to See Your Lips Move

Lessons in Following Jesus

What Would Happen If Beauty Ignored the Beast?

The two questions I am asked the most are "How do you stay so young looking?" and "What does your hair?" The hair thing is personal, so I will only discuss my secrets for staying so young looking. I consulted a beauty expert one time about a face-lift. After one session, he suggested a face removal. I decided that face-lifts, eye-lifts and nose-lifts were only for people who couldn't control their fork-lifts, so I worked on my one problem area: dry, cracked lips.

When I was a child, I had a severe problem with licking my lips. It was so severe I had a red ring around them. My lips looked like the north end of a southbound baboon. The only remedy that worked was petroleum jelly. I tried the grape flavor, but everywhere I went I had this eerie feeling I was being followed by toast.

The other secret of my youthful looks is grocery items—not eating them, wearing them. When you take a walk in the park, do small children point to your face and say things like, "That thing sure does need ironing"? According to skin-care specialists (whose motto is "I never met a face I liked"), you can use hot tea bags to help get rid of wrinkles. Important tip from personal experience: take the tea bags out of the boiling water *before* applying to your face.

For wrinkles around the mouth, you can eat yogurt sloppily. The yogurt combats the yeast infection that could be causing the wrinkles. Whatever dribbles will just fill in the cracks like putty. A remedy for wrinkles around the eyes is to cover them with cucumber or potato slices. They not only reduce the wrinkles, but they make great props when you want to scare the dog. Important tip from personal experience: do not let the neighbors see you chasing the dog around the house with vegetable slices attached to your eyes and yogurt drooling from your mouth.

The idea of beauty struggling with a beast is an old story, but it does cause us to ask some probing questions. Do we spend more time and money worrying about our outside beauty than we do our inside ugliness? Do we judge others on the beauty of their appearance or the ugliness of their circumstances? Do we find it difficult to accept people who are not like us?

Hard questions . . . but Jesus had the answer. The beauty in Jesus was that He spent time with the *beasts* of His day—the lepers, the publicans, the sinners, even His disciples.

Not a bad model for us to follow. There are *beasts* all around us who need to see the beauty of Christ. Unfortunately, we Christians, who are supposed to have the *beauty* within us, often choose to ignore the *beasts*, the sinners of the world. What a tragedy. For what could possibly take away the beastliness of the world but the beauty of Christ?

Living One Step before Water into Wine

I am traditional in my thinking. I like John Wayne movies, Sean Connery as James Bond, and fried chicken instead of baked. My wedding was pretty traditional, except for the part where Beverly's cousins threw possums instead of rice. There were the usual fifteen bridesmaids, two ministers, twelve acres of flowers, and one wedding coordinator, who, in her spare time, wrestled bulldogs.

That's why I brush off stories about couples getting married while parachuting or bungee jumping as just more people with the brain of a turnip. I did enjoy the story in the paper recently about a local wedding. It was performed with everyone on horseback inside a livestock barn. It gave new meaning to the phrase "surrounded by heifers." During the ceremony, the bride became nauseous. Never fear. In keeping with the Western motif, the minister presided over the ceremony from the back of the upchuck wagon.

2. Living One Step Before Water into Wine

Foreign weddings also have interesting traditions. On the night before a Chinese wedding, the bride bathes in water infused with grapefruit. Orange you glad they don't use prunes? In Greece, the parents of the bride and groom arrange for musicians to play music in their respective homes while they get ready for the ceremony. The festivities usually include heavy doses of drinking and dancing. Or was that in East Tennessee?

In Hispanic weddings, it is traditional for the bride to carry scented orange blossoms in her bouquet. In some West Texas weddings, it is not even customary for the bride to shower. Italian ceremonies have another unusual tradition. Two white doves are brought out and released to symbolize love and happiness. Weddings in remote areas of Arkansas have a similar ritual. To symbolize love and happiness, the parents of the bride release two hound dogs.

Jesus performed His first miracle at a wedding feast in Cana. The host ran out of wine, so Mary had a little talk with Jesus. (Jesus obviously did not have Baptists on His mind, or He would never have used wine for His first miracle.) We get so caught up in the wine that we brush over what Mary said to the servants after her discussion with Jesus. She simply told them to do whatever Jesus said. Instead of complaining, they brought out six pots full of water, and Jesus changed the water into the best wine anyone present had ever tasted.

That is the point of the miracle. Jesus can take the ordinary and make it extraordinary, if we let Him. But we have to take the first step. The problem is that we gripe and complain about other people doing this or doing that, and we don't ever take the time to give what we have to Jesus. He can take whatever water we have and turn it into wine. The first step is letting Him change our whine into water.

Some Days Are Diamonds, Some Days You Hear Elvis in the Attic

You know it's not going to be a good day when you get out of the bed at five in the morning and step on your Chihuahua. In my case, it was Tiny. In all fairness, I guess the day was none too promising for Tiny, either, even though she is one of those industrial-strength hypersensitive female Chihuahuas who wears her feelings on her sleeve and cries at the drop of a cat. She cries after I reach into the dog biscuit box and raise my hand to toss her a biscuit. After squashing my Chihuahua, the rest of the day went downhill from there.

There are others who have had worse days. A story out of Romania detailed a bad day for a bear and a man. The man was checking his sheep. A bear came out of the woods and started chasing him. The man fell and broke his leg. He thought he was dead. His pet Pekingese had another idea. The dog attacked the bear and chased him into the woods, returning safely an hour later, strutting like John Travolta in *Saturday Night Fever*.

The bear and the man had the same problem. They had to go back to the den and tell their buddies about their encounter with a Pekingese, a dog that looks like someone drew a face on a hairy pancake. The man learned his lesson. He is no longer going to check (√) his sheep, just mark them with an "x".

A man in South Korea complained of a headache. He went to the doctor, and X-rays revealed a two-inch nail embedded in his skull. He did not remember how it happened. I may be a typical male and not notice when Beverly moves a couch from one wall to another, but I'm pretty sure I would remember a meeting between my head and a nail.

A man in Texas found a box of old, dusty recordings in his attic. He claimed they were amateur recordings of Elvis Presley. When told by experts it was not the voice of Elvis, he went into an uncontrollable frenzy. You know what happened: he was all shook up.

A woman in Israel accidentally swallowed a cockroach. (Is there any other way to swallow a cockroach?) She tried to retrieve it with a fork and swallowed the fork. She is fine. The subsequent surgery was successful. Doctors were told simply to look at the X-rays and turn right when they got to the fork in the roach.

It's that way in life. Some days, there's a song in your heart and a zip in your step. The next day, there's a fork in your stomach and a nail in your head. How do you react? Sometimes I don't do so well. When someone tries to cheer me up by quoting Scripture, my first reaction is to grab a Bible and throw it at them. But with my luck, the pages would fall open to "This is the day the LORD has made. We will rejoice and be glad in it" (Psalm 118:24 NLT).

7

Rightfully so. This really is the day the Lord has made. It is provided for us by Jesus Himself. He had one of His days end with nails, not in His head but in His hands and feet. He could have avoided it but instead chose to die. It was not a good day.

When I think of that, my day is really not so bad, and I ain't nothin' but a hound dog for my cryin' all the time. I need to wake up every morning and decide it's now or never. I'm going to live this day for God. He really does love me tender.

Christ, Crest, Cheese, and Choices

I have just completed my great American right to vote. Actually, the great American voting part only took about one minute. Most of my rights were spent standing in line for two hours listening to the man behind me drone on about the candidates of his particular party. His breath smelled like his mouth had been housing a school of flounder.

I'm not saying the line was long, but it was moving so slowly snails were having races around me. There was a pregnant woman in the line ahead of me. When she came out, her child was walking. When I finally got to the booth and threw open the curtain, I was greeted by the choices of 283 names for 63 positions.

There were presidents, vice presidents, senators, congressmen, state senators, and a million local elections. Being a proud American who takes voting seriously and studies the platform of each candidate, I voted for the first person listed or the one whose name had the most vowels.

Voting is not the only area where I am bombarded with choices. I went to the grocery store to get a few simple items like toothpaste and cheese. It was another American right shredded to pieces. You can't get just toothpaste or just cheese anymore. There are 127 brands of toothpaste, and each one does something different.

Toothpaste can now whiten my teeth, freshen my breath (flounder man could have used it), strengthen my gums, desensitize my teeth, and control my tartar. The only tartar I thought I had was the sauce for the flounder. And I didn't even know I had sensitive teeth. I looked in the mirror one morning and simply made a passing comment about them being yellow, and they started crying.

It's not much better with cheese. You can't get just cheese anymore. It comes shredded, sliced, cubed, processed, fat free, milk free, preservative free, and born free. It can come from buffalo, camels, goats, and cows (oh my!), as long as their milk has curdled. You know the milk has curdled if you have to drink it with a fork. And these days, you have to buy cheese that has been inoculated. You know it's inoculated because it can't walk a straight line.

We face choices every day. Some are small and meaningless, while others are more important. They may range from what we buy at the grocery store to a decision at work that may compromise our integrity. Your child comes to you needing your attention. How do you respond? Your spouse comes to you needing your time. What do you do? A friend hurts you with his words. How do you react? The man behind you is tailgating you on the highway. Do you control yourself?

Jesus faced choices every day too. Before He began His ministry, Satan tempted Him with choices. Jesus chose God's way each time. And anytime we have a choice between love and hate or love and anger, we must choose love. Jesus said, "A new command I give you: Love one another. As I have loved you, so you must love one another" (John 13:34). When it comes to loving people, we don't seem to have a choice.

When Old Sailors Die, Do They Just Fade Aweigh?

There are some things in life that will always be a mystery. A family in Sweden had just sat down to a nice quiet dinner of sardines and reindeer when the doorbell rang. The father looked through the peephole but could not tell who it was, although he could hear heavy breathing. They looked out the window and discovered a moose at the front door. I have two questions. Why can you never see anything through a peephole? And how did the moose know to use the doorbell?

A family in Greenland had just sat down for a quiet dinner of sardines and polar bear when a military tank came crashing through the front door. An eyewitness reported that just before the tank smashed through the front door, she heard the tank sergeant yell out, "Avon calling!" Again, I have two questions. Why do people eat so many sardines? And when did Avon start using tanks to improve sales?

Germany also has a few problems. Toads, for no apparent reason, are swelling and blowing up. Experts are trying to unravel the mystery of the exploding toads. They can't figure out why a perfectly good toad can be minding its own business one minute, and the next minute he's airborne in five thousand different directions.

One expert said it could be a defense mechanism because of aggressive crows. Another scientist said, "This is such a huge mess, we are going to have to call a toad truck." I have two more questions. How many exploding toads do you have to see before you become an expert? And why do Germans make such good chocolate but horrible puns?

As if the toad incident wasn't strange enough, a cow walked into a bank, made a few turns, and walked out. Most employees agreed on one thing. The cow could make all the withdrawals she wanted. They just didn't want her making any deposits.

I love mystery movies and mystery books. One of my favorite television shows was *Murder, She Wrote.* On each episode, a murder is committed, and Jessica Fletcher solves it. One of my favorite board games is Clue. A murder is committed, and the object of the game is to guess correctly the suspect, the weapon, and the room. It is a mystery until the end of the game.

There is another mystery in the game of life. Paul says in Romans 5:8, "God showed his great love for us by sending Christ to die for us while we were still sinners" (NLT). I can't understand that kind of love. As in the game of Clue, there is a killing in the game of Life. Christ killed sin. He did it on a hill . . . with a cross . . . and that is no mystery.

As to why God could love me so much as to send His only Son to die for me, I don't have a clue. I guess I will have to wait until the end of the game.

It's OK to Sing to Mushrooms, but Never Goose a Moose

Some things just don't make sense. A man was hiking in a remote area of New Jersey and suffered multiple leg fractures when he fell trying to escape from an angry goose. Two questions begged to be asked. Why was he on foot in New Jersey? And what could possibly make a goose angry? Detectives concluded the agnostic goose became agitated when the born-again hiker tried to place a bumper sticker on the goose's rear end that read, "Honk if you love Jesus!"

Here's one to tell your grandchildren. Slices of toast bearing the resemblance of Michael Jackson are being sold on eBay. I've seen the pictures. They look more like Diana Ross. This, and a series of unfortunately similar events, has prompted the city of New York to change the inscription on the Statue of Liberty. It will soon read, "Give me your tired, your poor, your stupid, your brain-dead masses, your lug nut from a 1972 Chevrolet Vega, and your toast, and I will sell it on eBay."

6. It's OK to Sing to Mushrooms, but Never Goose a Moose

A couple in Norway was taking a leisurely Sunday drive when a moose landed on the roof of their car. The "flying" moose evidently had been startled in the woods above the highway and took off running, unable to stop at the edge. In outdoor language, startling a moose is called "moose goosing"—not something you want to do. Having just finished a few Norwegian drinks, the couple panicked, thinking they had killed Rudolph. The moral of this story is no place is safe if a goosed moose is on the loose.

A man in Prague listens to mushrooms and then composes music based on his encounters. I can just picture the man walking in the park with his grandson. "Granddaddy, what do you do in your spare time?" "Well, son, I put a mushroom in my ear and sing to it." "Granddaddy, do you mind if I don't take you to show-and-tell?" The moral of this story is if you want to get music out of something besides the radio, then listen to a trumpeter swan, a hummingbird, a fiddler crab, or a C turtle.

There were similar reactions to Jesus. When it came time to feed the multitudes one day, the disciples wondered where the food would come from. Jesus looked at the disciples and said, "You feed them" (a loose translation of Matthew 14:16). The disciples probably got that "Yeah right, when moose fly and mushrooms sing" look on their faces. When next we saw the disciples, they were picking up the leftovers.

Jesus healed a blind man. The people didn't understand. It didn't make sense to the blind man either. When asked about it, all he could say was, "One thing I do know. I was blind but now I see!" (John 9:25). I've never sung to a mushroom or goosed a moose, but I agree with the blind man.

Maybe that's our problem: we spend too much time trying to figure out God. And if we do that often enough, we are going to miss out on a lot of God's work and run the risk of spending our lives with the disciples . . . just picking up leftovers.

The Perils of "Round John Virgin" and "Gladly the Cross-Eyed Bear"

*C*ommunication is a wonderful invention. It has brought together such diverse personalities as rock musicians and dentists through unintelligible grunts. A dentist can understand every word you say even though tooth parts are flying around your mouth in all directions, a grappling hook large enough to snag a whale is digging out leftover chicken between your teeth, and a subatomic vacuum similar to those used to gut a mackerel is sucking out all of your bodily fluids.

To prove he understands you, the dentist keeps asking questions even though your gums are so dead your lower lip has sunk to the floor. Wives, because of their exposure to rock musicians and dentists, are able to take this valuable information into the marital relationship and interpret their husbands' grunts. The conversation goes something like this: The unintelligible husband says, "Honjkwr, whlcdr ts gkt retoem ctnlor?" The patient wife hears, "Honey, where is the remote control?" and answers, "It's on the floor under your dirty socks!"

Another example of great communication was colonial America, with the most notable incident involving Paul Revere and his Midnight Ride, where he gave the garbled and famously misunderstood message: "One in my hand, tooth in my seat." One night Revere discovered some English grandmothers putting up vegetables in a cabin near Lexington. Known as a practical joker, he jumped on his horse and started to ride like the wind, but instead he fell like a tree. His horse was still tied to the post. After untying his horse, he remounted and rode away exclaiming, in a heavy Bahston accent, "The British are canning! The British are canning!"

Well, the minutemen had hearing problems from listening to their wives badger them about dirty socks on the floor. They misunderstood Revere, fired on a group of English dentists, and the War for Independence (subtitled The War for White Wigs and Tight Pants) was on.

We all chuckle when we hear children tell us what they hear when we sing hymns. They hear "round John virgin" instead of "round yon virgin," and they picture "gladly the cross-eyed bear" instead of "gladly the cross I'd bear." We laugh at our children, but we adults sometimes do the same thing with the words of Jesus.

He said, "For God so loved *the* world," not *some* of the world (John 3:16). He also said, "I came that they may have *life,* and have it abundantly" (John 10:10 NRSV), not "I came that you may have *strife.*" We listen to the words, but we seldom hear Him speak, ultimately bringing shame to what He lived and died for.

Why can't we be more like Jesus? We know the ground is level at the foot of the cross, meaning Jesus died for everyone. But the ground is also level at the manger, meaning He *lived* for everyone. Jesus loved people, and He treated them all equally. Why can't we do the shame? Excuse me—I meant to say, *same.* It seems we've already mastered the shame.

Does Your Ship of Servanthood Ever Run Aground?

I haven't been involved in politics very much, other than buying a few votes in my drive to be elected captain of the safety patrol in sixth grade. (My winning slogan was "Don't be a slab; vote for Babb.") The United States Senate discusses many life-changing topics every day, but as Johann Sebastian used to say in mad moments of musical frustration, "This is the straw that baroque the camel's Bach."

Several years ago, the senators spent valuable time discussing whether to grant Lake Champlain in Vermont "Great Lake" status. I am totally against this because it would mess up the acrostic I learned while sleeping through geography class. The acrostic H.O.M.E.S. helped me learn the names of the five Great Lakes—Huron, Ontarius, Michael, Ernie, and Superior . . . or was that the Jackson Five? There are other important issues they need to be discussing, like making it illegal for people to use bad grammar or say "chimley" (instead of "chimney") while being interviewed on live television.

There is a burning question that has bothered pickerel, carp, and shad (Is that a Dallas law firm?) for years. What exactly makes a Great Lake? There are several requirements. One of them is the number of fishing lures and aluminum cans on the bottom. Another is how many varieties of dead fish are floating on the surface. Of course, the deciding factor is the amount of water each contains, currently the equivalent of five Lamaze classes.

Let me describe their bigness . . . um, the lakes, not the classes. If you took all the ministers of music in the world and laid them side by side across the lake, you could call it "Bridge Over Trebled Water" . . . and then more dead fish would float to the surface. What mercifully ended the senators' discussion was the realization that if they added Lake Champlain, they would have to add a "C" to H.O.M.E.S. The only word they could come up with was "M.C.S.H.O.E." It was ruled out of order because it was already being used as the name for a tough new burger at McDonald's.

As important as this discussion was, it pales in comparison to the debate as to what makes a person great. Some people's lives are covered with the lures of wealth, power, and fame in their attempt to catch the elusive fish called "greatness." Jesus had a different twist on the subject when He equated greatness with servanthood. The road to greatness is paved with servanthood but has wealth, power, and fame as potholes.

The key to the status of greatness is in not seeking it. The Great Lakes are not man-made, and neither is greatness. It does not matter how many committees we serve on, how much money we have, or how important we are in the community. Unlike a lake, our greatness is not measured by how big we are but how much of ourselves we give away in showing others how big God is.

CRAZY THE LORD!

Hallelu, Hallelu, Hallelu, Hallelujah, Crazy the Lord!

I have seen some crazy things in my lifetime. I watched the ending of the California-Stanford football game in 1982 as California won on the last play of the game. They received the kickoff and went right down the field with a play called something like "Let's lateral this ball to whatever Cal player is nearest, for a total of seventy-five laterals, and run through half the student body and the entire Stanford band the last ten yards before scoring the touchdown and knocking down an unsuspecting and somewhat perplexed trombone player."

I have observed what I believe to be crazy people bungee jumping off of buildings and bridges. Had I not watched it on television, I would not have believed it. These people have no dough in their biscuits. My Chihuahua's brain went out for pizza and never came back, but at least she quit bungee jumping.

In junior high and high school, I was not normal like I am now. I looked in my high-school yearbook to see what they said about me. Some favorites were: "You're a real crazy guy. Stephanie"; "Martin, Baby, you have made Trigonometry much better than it would have been. You are a riot! Luv, Debbie"; "Hey, Groovy, We were crazy in American History. Keep Groovin, Rick"; "You're really a crazy guy, and I'm sorry I've been so rude to you every time I tell you to shut up. Good luck, Margie"; and "Say Martin! You are a real cool, groovy, mellow fellow, crazy cat. Reginald."

Some others were: "Trig has been a lot of fun. Love, Janet"; "Just think! Before this year I didn't even know you. Now I know you and really don't know if I missed anything. Love ya, Carolyn"; "Biology has been crazy. You are really normal. I lied. Stay crazy. Love ya, Capi"; "You're one of the craziest, most lovable guys I've ever met. Love, Lisa." Moral of the story? Trigonometry can drive you crazy, unless you approach it from the right angle.

I guess crazy is a relative term, its true definition a product of one's perspective. I was reminded of this several years ago after a worship service. We had sung the chorus, "Hallelu, hallelu, hallelu, hallelujah, Praise ye the Lord!" A church member informed me that her six-year-old son, Lincoln, misunderstood and sang, "Hallelu, hallelu, hallelu, hallelujah, Crazy the Lord!"

I smiled but then I thought about all the things Jesus did that, based on one's point of view, might be considered a little bit crazy. He preferred servanthood to kingship, respected His parents, befriended sinners, touched lepers, commanded demons, calmed a raging sea, associated with taxgatherers, stood up to sanctimonious religious leaders, and forgave His enemies.

Sounds a little crazy to me. And even crazier, He expects us to follow in His footsteps. He is the same yesterday, today, and tomorrow. To borrow the words of a Paul Simon song, Jesus is "still crazy after all these years."

Where Would a Cow Put a Pocket Pager?

orget the presidential and vice-presidential debates, and ignore the price of oil. We need to talk about cows. Cows are wonderful creatures. If they are not eating, they are sleeping. They make great college freshmen. Cows are more than just hamburgers waiting to happen. They are the root of wonderful words like coward, which means "in the direction of a cow."

Cows also provide opportunities for humorous news stories. At one California institute, scientists are experimenting with placing cows in a specially designed bovine greenhouse to study their emissions . . . um, the cows' emissions, not the scientists'. Personally, I don't want to be sitting in a restaurant and eating a meal that was once studied because of its emissions.

Another story (probably just a rumor) involved a small ship that was sunk by a flying cow. It turns out that some fun-loving air force guys threw a cow out the door of their plane because she was getting rowdy. The cow had no parachute and did not yell "Geronimoo!" In reality, things got out of hand on the plane while the airmen were playing a game of high-steaks poker.

Farmers in Japan are also experimenting. They are calling their cows to chow time by equipping them with pocket pagers and calling the cow's pager on a cell phone. That is fine, but what happens if the farmer gets the operator? "I'm sorry, operator, I was just trying to call my cow." What's the name of the phone company, Cow Bell?

The cows have been trained, upon hearing the beepers, to stop grazing and head for the food. The farmers also discovered that playing music over a loudspeaker called the cows to the feedlot. Interestingly enough, some of the dairy cattle, after hearing rap music, quit giving milk and began giving sour cream. The worst was when they played Bach with a large church pipe organ. This, of course, caused the cows to give organic milk. The music system actually worked pretty well until some of the cows grazed too far away to hear the speakers.

We can learn a lot from cows. Sometimes our verbal emissions can pollute the spiritual atmosphere around us. We seem to ignore its effect on people. Cows' nourishment needs are simple, and so are ours, spiritually. The "feedlot" for a Christian is to act like Jesus did, to love people like Jesus did, to be like Jesus. What do we do when God tries to call us back to the feedlot? Do we go immediately, or do we just look up momentarily and then continue grazing?

God is calling to each of us. He is calling us to get back to the basics. He is calling us back to the "feedlot." As Christians, we are a family, connected through God. He wants us to be prepared to love and minister to those around us and to reach people in our community for Jesus Christ. God is calling. How will we respond? Are we going to answer, or have we grazed too far away to hear the Music?

Chapter 2:
You Can't Let Sleeping Dogs Lie if You Let the Cat Out of the Bag

Lessons in Life from Non-Humans

You May Not Like Its Song, but That's No Reason to Kill a Mockingbird

I do not consider myself to be an avid bird watcher. I like to watch birds out my back window, but not the avids. Serious bird watchers, called "birders," can be walking through the woods and easily spot a yellow-rumped warbler (which is also a pretty good description of my daughter when she was two months old) or a bristle-thighed curlew (which come to think of it, was my grandmother's nickname).

They also have no difficulty spotting the lesser goldfinch. It is easily recognizable because of its chant, "We're number two!" I'm more of a birdbrain. I know just certain kinds of birds like robins, sparrows, cardinals, orioles, Larry, and Big.

When the governor of Tennessee was inaugurated several years ago, there was a serious problem with starlings in the plaza. His aides had difficulty dealing with them, and there was a huge flap. They were roosting in the magnolia trees . . . um, the starlings, not his aides. His aides were roosting near the lobbyists. Evidently, starlings love trees with substantial foliage to break the wind. There seems to be more than an ample supply of that in government.

There are other interesting facts about birds that have nothing to do with wind-breaking foliage. The harpy eagle of South America (similar to the groucho and zeppo eagle) feeds on monkeys. For these birds, there really is no more fun in life than a barrel of monkeys.

The American egret is unique because of Nathan Hale, who said, "I egret that I have but one life to give for my country." The Montezuma quail is most famous for its revenge on freshly washed parked cars, while the Chihuahuan raven of Southwest Texas is known for its quick temper, especially if you try to take away its biscuit. It also makes numerous stops in flight to mark its territory.

The long-eared owl is relatively silent. According to one expert, it sometimes gives low moaning hoots, sort of like the bass section in the church choir. A more down-home bird is the red-necked grebe, easily recognizable because it always wears a T-shirt that says, "I'm with stupid."

The secretary bird of Africa kills and eats poisonous snakes and lizards, but not before she types their letters and makes them coffee. The most unique of all is the sandwich tern. It feeds on liverwurst, from which we get the phrase "took a tern for the wurst."

We can learn a lot from birds. Every bird has a song to sing and has no trouble sharing it. Listen to the varied sounds of the thrush, the robin, the mockingbird, the cardinal, and others. Think of how incomplete nature's symphony would be without the singing of the birds. Even those who aren't songbirds are in the choir. Someone once said, "A bird in the hand is worth two in the bush." That may be a catchy proverb, but it doesn't work that way when taking gifts. Gifts were meant to be shared.

Every Christian has a gift. Are you using it in the church or community, or are you holding on to it? God's symphony is incomplete without every Christian singing his song and sharing his gift. Besides, a spiritual gift, like a bird in the hand, will soon die if not set free.

Is there a place of service in your church where you need to be singing your song? If you are not singing your song by using your spiritual gift, then you are living a Christianity that is simply for the birds. Don't duck your responsibility. Take your tern, and stop robin yourself of the opportunity to serve God. You won't egret it.

Why Do Chihuahuas Chase Bees?

T hrough the years my family has survived infestations of mice, possums, squirrels, ants, horseflies, worms, goldfish, dance recitals, one psychedelic experiment with orange walls in the late 1970s, and one nightmarish episode with hamsters. So far, we have avoided the frogs and locusts.

Our family's latest sojourn into the land of Pharaoh involves wasps. These are no ordinary wasps. They are Jurassic wasps. They don't just sting; they carry cordless drills. They are best controlled at night when they are in their nest listening to their favorite singer, Sting.

One method of fighting the wasps is wasp spray. I could actually see their little mouths opening to drink the spray. They loved it. It was like hosing down a Labrador retriever. Finally, after enough toxic spray to take down a water buffalo, they succumbed. Of course, everything within twenty feet of the back door was dripping with toxic spray. It looked like an alien had exploded.

Another school of thought on wasping endorses the use of dogs. Some dogs are great for hunting. Beagles and political candidates chase rabbits, bull terriers shoot the bull, rat terriers kill rats, and Moscow watchdogs just kill time.

My Chihuahuas are good waspers. Why? They have no fear . . . and they have no brains. One of them even chases bees. They jump at every crawling or flying insect, and because their intelligence level ranks just below guacamole dip, they bark and nip constantly at the wasp, driving him crazy. It is casually entertaining for the wasp, but he does eventually become irritated. That's when he is most vulnerable.

While the Chihuahuas are barking and nipping, I jump in with both swatters swinging. At this point, two things can happen: I can kill the wasp, or I can miss the wasp and hit the Chihuahuas. There is something comical about watching swatted and somewhat surprised Chihuahuas tuck their curly little tails and dive under the nearest bed.

What about you? Have you met any wasps lately? Oh, not the physical species but the spiritual kind. Have you been stung by the circumstances of life? Were you unprepared to deal with the pain and suffering that followed? There is hope.

There are two ways a person can attack spiritual W.A.S.P.S. One is by wearing the Worldly Apparel of Selfishness, Pride, and Stubbornness. This person approaches life for what he can get out of it and depends only on himself. He is like a Chihuahua chasing a bee. He knows he might get stung, but he doesn't care. When he is attacked by life, he has no defense.

The other view uses the Whole Armor Shield of faith, Prayer, and Sword of the Spirit. This person approaches life as a gift and depends on God every day, not just during the bad times.

If we have truly been *W.A.S.P.*ed in the blood of Christ, we will take the second approach and be better prepared to deal with the "wasps" that come into our lives unexpectedly, from any direction. In the end, we can even join with the apostle Paul in asking, "O death, where is thy sting?" (1 Corinthians 15:55 KJV).

Does God's Plan Have Roaming Charges?

It seems that no matter how much we sing the song, buffalo no longer feel at home on the range. They are wandering, and according to a recent newspaper article, three of them have wandered into our own peaceful little county. This is an outrage! I thought buffalo only roamed in Montana (state mottoes: "What's That Smell?" and "Watch Your Step!"). What happened? Did they take a wrong turn in Missoula? (Then again, who hasn't taken a wrong turn in Missoula?) Local officials decided the buffalo were just here for a poker game. The place where they apparently bedded down was covered with buffalo chips. Personally, I think they were here for a belated celebration of our bisontennial.

A headline in a different paper read, "Hundreds of Wild Bison Hazed Back into Yellowstone National Park." The outrage within me mounts. I thought hazing was outlawed. What did they do, make them do push-ups in front of the girls' dorm wearing beanies and short pants? One other headline read, "Buffalo Killed for Roaming." Of course, this made the rest of the buffalo make immediate changes to their cell phone plans.

Along with roaming bison, there are reports of wandering moose. Two adult moose with radio collars wandered into Wisconsin from Michigan. Evidently, their radio collars were set on rock-'n'-roll, and they wanted polka. They had been part of the reintroduction of moose to the Upper Peninsula. It went like this: "Mr. Peninsula, meet Mr. Moose."

In another story, the headline read, "Man Shoots Charging Moose." The moose was quoted as saying, "Next time I'll use cash." The man was charged with a moosedemeanor.

One story from Norway reported that wandering Norwegian moose are eating fermenting fruit and becoming intoxicated. You don't want to mess with a juiced moose. Locals were told that if they were confronted by a drunken moose, they should "clap and see how it reacts." What? If I'm approached by a pickled moose, I'm supposed to applaud? What will it do, break into a chorus of show tunes?

Evidently moose and buffalo don't do too well when they wander away from home. It reminds me of the Hebrew people in the Old Testament as they wandered in the wilderness, far from home. They didn't fare too well. They found slavery. What about Jonah? He tried to wander away from God. He found a whale. It also reminds me of the prodigal son who wandered into a far country. He was so hungry that he longed to eat with the pigs.

What is home for the Christian but living within the protection of God's will? It's easy for us to look at people in the Bible and wonder how they could fail God, but we fail God every day when we wander from His will. We just don't usually find ourselves eating with pigs or looking for food inside a whale.

I wonder sometimes if God's plan for our lives includes roaming charges. That's OK. I understand He has an extensive grace period.

Nothing Brightens a Monday Like a Possum in the Preschool

f Monday mornings in a church office could be calm and un-
eventful, I thought this would surely be one. I was working the
day watch, performing simple minister of education stuff (Is
that an oxymoron?) like counting paper plates, sharpening pen-
cils, and looking for leaks in all the wrong places.

The stillness of the morning was shattered by what sounded like
a dozen coyotes giving birth to porcupines without epidurals. These
were normal sounds in a church office. A few seconds later, there was
a knock at my door. It was one of our preschool teachers.

For fear of embarrassment and total humiliation, I will not use
her real name. Shannon (not her real name and not the daughter
of Van and Susan) was visibly shaken and very much stirred. She
asked me the question every minister of education, if he survives
long enough in the church business, will eventually hear: "Can
you come get this possum out of my classroom?"

My first question was how a possum could get into our pre-school. Every applicant has to fill out a form and pay a deposit. He had done neither. He was in our preschool illegally. Once I got over the initial shock of having illegal possums in our preschool, I began my plan of attack.

I needed a weapon. I went down the hall to our possum armament closet to see what was available. Being a dutiful advocate of Vacation Bible School, I armed myself with the Christian flag. My only concern was whether the possum would remember the stand-up/sit-down chords.

I entered the room cautiously, peering left and right. I was concerned about the possum but also wary of the ramifications of someone seeing me waving a Christian flag over my head trying to bring down a possum. It was like a scene from *Kung Fu Meets the Crusades.*

Sue, another brave teacher, calmly grabbed a small fishing net and slammed it down over the possum. I gently put the flag aside, took the possum from Sue, and carried it to the vacant lot across the street. We had survived what seemed like an impossumble situation.

That was only one of several meetings I have had with possums over the years. It was the only church-related incident and the only one that ended positively for the possum. After the ordeal, I checked my Bible concordance but could not find any verses in the Bible that mentioned possums. Were none of the writers from Arkansas?

I did remember a few words of Jesus in Matthew about prayer being able to move mountains. Prayer would surely work on possums, but I never gave it a chance. I wonder sometimes if we as Christians don't find ourselves in some situations that seem hopeless or even impossible, but we forget to use prayer as a weapon.

Prayer is our ultimate weapon, and with it we can wade into any situation fully armed. Luke 11:10 says, "For everyone who asks receives, and he who seeks finds, and to him who knocks it will be opened" (NKJV). Remember, Jesus also said something like, "With God, all things are possumble."

Living Somewhere Between Horse Fly and Fruit Fly

We had an invasion of flies in our house several years ago. Lest you think these were common house flies, let me exaggerate. These were Desperate House Flies. These were horse flies, of the suborder Brachycera, which is Latin for "large bloodsucking creatures with multicolored eyes," a description not to be confused with agents for professional athletes. These flies were prunes with wings, large enough to carry off small animals and make bunk beds out of No-Pest Strips. They didn't just buzz; they carried vacuum cleaners and siphon hoses.

Some of them had as many as three mandibles, sometimes referred to as the Mandible Sisters: Barbara, Louise, and Erlene. One daring dipteran even had the audacity to fly so close I could hear him humming the theme song to *Top Gun*. They used our fly swatters as trampolines. There were so many fly-by swattings that our living room looked like an Olympic badminton contest on steroids. And there was just way too much pupating going on for my comfort level.

During a lull in the bombardment one day, I took time out for a body count. At that point there were ninety-three dead flies, one unsuspecting moth (whose final expression of surprise was, "Why me?"), and one wounded Chihuahua. She was simply a victim of bad aim but with an even more earnest look of surprise and a few hundred degrees of agitation thrown in.

Things with fur, wings, tails, or more than two eyes always manage to find our house. I think it is either through our membership in the Hitchcockian "Rodent of the Month" Club or our five-star listing in the *Mobil Pest Travel Guide*. During that particular "you-must-be-related-to-Pharaoh" plague, my only reprieve was the discovery of a birds' nest being built outside the bathroom window sill.

One night after chasing a battalion of the Jedi flies into the bathroom, I heard the mama bird busily building her nest and singing her song. Life goes on in spite of the flies. For a few moments, I forgot about the flies.

Unfortunately, there are too many people in this world who would make great horse flies. They don't like you, and everything you do annoys them. No particular reason—some people just seem to enjoy being contrary, so they buzz from one topic to another and from one person to another, sucking the life and the enthusiasm out of every room they enter.

What can you do? You keep doing what you should always do. You exhibit the fruit of the Spirit. People like that aren't going to change. And you must be careful not to let them change you.

We make a choice every day in how we are going to treat the people around us. We can buzz with the flies, or we can sing with the birds. Paul tells us in Ephesians to "Walk in the way of love, just as Christ loved us and gave himself up for us as a fragrant offering and sacrifice to God" (5:2 TNIV).

Share the fruit of the Spirit. As for me, my world just seems to be a happier and more fragrant place when I allow the music of the birds to drown out the disharmony of the flies. Don't be a horse fly . . . be a fruit fly.

You Can Chase a Tuna, but It Won't Help Your Eyesight

There are certain events and phenomena no one, including Larry, Darrell, and Darrell, has ever really explained to my satisfaction.

As of 1973, there were more than five thousand man-made objects in space; 2,736 of them came from a garage sale. Castor oil is used as a lubricant in jet planes; the hard part is getting the planes to swallow it without making a face. A sneeze can travel as fast as one hundred miles per hour. Hmm. Let's say I am planning a trip to a destination one hundred miles away, and I plan to drive fifty miles per hour. If I stick my head out the window and sneeze when I leave, my sneeze will arrive exactly thirty minutes before I do.

Animals provide us with the most interesting phenomena. A tuna can swim one hundred miles in a single day, two hundred if he is being chased by a loaf of bread, some chopped eggs, and one tablespoon of sweet pickle relish. Salmon in the Northwest literally swim upstream, figuratively if they form a committee to investigate an alternate route.

Dolphins communicate through a series of high-pitched shrieks, similar to a teenage girl who discovers a spider in her sheets. A good milking cow will give six thousand quarts of milk a year, but she is not happy about it. To escape its enemies, a squid will put up a smoke screen. To get out of cleaning his room, a teenager can do even better.

When a hippopotamus exerts itself or gets angry, it exudes red sweatlike mucus through its skin, very similar to fans at Vanderbilt football games. It is a little-known fact that owls, if raised in the wrong environment, can turn bad. They have been seen screaming obscenities out the window while driving an automobile. Scientists refer to this phenomenon as a drive-by hooting.

In addition to these oddities, there is another one I don't understand. Why is it so difficult for us to accept people as they are when it was so easy for Jesus? He ministered to all people, no matter how they looked or where they lived. He even loves me, in spite of my flaws. Like the words of an old gospel song, "He looked beyond my fault and saw my need." Jesus constantly performed little intentional acts of blindness.

If we want to be like Jesus, we shouldn't spend so much time and energy dwelling on a person's negative characteristics or gender or skin color that we forget about the soul underneath. Maybe there is a good reason that person on the street doesn't look so good or smell so nice. Have we ever stopped to find out?

Do we ever take the time to ask a troubled friend at work or church how things are going? Do we send a note or a card? Do we get involved in feeding the homeless? Do we care? Jesus said, "That is why I tell these stories, because people see what I do, but they don't really see . . . and they don't understand" (Matthew 13:13 NLT).

Until we begin to see life through little intentional acts of blindness, our sight will never really be made whole . . . and that is one difficult-to-explain phenomenon.

lesson 17

Another Martin, Another Door, Another Diet of Worms

I should have been prepared. But how could I? I was never a Boy Scout. The only motto I live by is "Be repaired!" It was a simple phone call from North Carolina to Tennessee, to check on my family—sort of like Ward Cleaver calling to check on June, Wally, and the Beav. But then I heard the six words that would make any father faint: "Mom, tell Dad about the worms!"

Having previously survived a rather scary squirrel safari and an even more frightening family fly fest, I received this news with less than a cheerful heart. In fact, on my list of favorite things to hear over the phone, it ranks right up there with "Someone left the hamster cage open" and "I think the possum in the wall had babies!"

There must be a Statue of Liberty, visible only to the insect/animal kingdom, in our yard that reads, "Bring your huddled ani-

44

mals, your teeming insects, and all of their gross friends and leave them here at the Babb house. This is the same man who, as a greasy-haired junior-high kid, stuck straight pins into innocent dead beetles and roaches for a science project in 1966!"

Back to the worms. Beverly was showing our friends, Vernon and Rhea-Anne, around our new home. She opened up the door to our walk-out basement, and there they were. A bazillion tiny wormlike creatures had attached themselves to our back door. Maybe their plane was rerouted, or maybe they all simultaneously decided our back door was the safest place to avoid the early bird. Whatever the reason, there they were.

At the foot of the door lay the carcass of a dead rat, compliments of our neighbor's cat. Our neighbor's cat is an excellent hunter. Being a neighborly cat, he sometimes deposits his kill at our back door. I guess he thinks it will taste better than what we normally eat.

If you've watched enough episodes of *CSI*, you know that dead objects, left unattended, will attract two things: a black 2005 Hummer and tiny wormlike creatures. We got the creatures. It wasn't a discussion of Martin Luther's beliefs at the Diet of Worms; this *was* a diet of worms. Vernon graciously insisted that as long as we live, we should never ever invite him over for dinner.

Have you ever had one of those days, weeks, or even months where everything that could possibly go wrong actually did? Did it make you wonder if all the bad circumstances in life got together and decided to focus their annual meeting around you? Don't ever let anyone tell you Christians can't have bad days, weeks, months, or even years. We do, and for us it is a test of faith. After Jesus quieted the storm on the Sea of Galilee, He looked at the frightened disciples and asked, "Where is your faith?" (Luke 8:25).

We have a tendency to forget that God promised never to leave us, no matter the circumstances. Martin Luther was right in his critical stand on justification by faith. Faith is the key; but when we turn that key to let God in, we also open the door to the storms, the flies, and the worms of life.

It is a test of our faith. If we choose to dine with Jesus, we better expect the worms. Just don't expect them to stay.

lesson 18

Praying Hands and Swooping Owls

I try to live a simple life. Except for several Chihuahua emergencies involving a bumblebee, a fly swatter, a mousetrap, and a rubber glove, it is a quiet and sheltered life. And with the possible exception of a bizarre and somewhat overpublicized incident in college years ago involving a hot-dog pizza, a nighttime visit to a bronze statue, a powerful set of headlights, and an obviously stunned driver, I am seldom visibly shaken.

Recently, I was reminded of something that happened at Vanderbilt University several years ago. If you have a sensitive stomach, stop reading here. If you have preschoolers, do not let them read any further unless you have access to a trained child psychologist or SpongeBob SquarePants. Once upon a time, there were swooping owls at Vanderbilt—not to be confused with the more docile Rice Owls of Houston, who have lost their swoop.

If I am taking a casual, $100,000-a-semester stroll through the campus of Vanderbilt University, I should not have to worry about swooping owls. Rumor has it, the owls were turned loose on the campus to control the squirrel population but started attacking the students instead. One student said, "I guess my head looked like a squirrel!" This is an outrage! First, I want to know why there was a perfectly good rumor going around and no Baptists were notified. Second, are the squirrels and owls paying full tuition?

Finally, I want to know why the students look like squirrels. These students will eventually graduate, own corporations, and cheer for Florida when they play Tennessee. Another eyewitness said, "It attacked a security officer near Divinity. We looked through the area but did not see any nests." Well, of course not! You can't see security officer nests with the naked eye! You must have highly sophisticated night-vision goggles with doughnut-infused lenses.

The owls were nuisances, but everyone should be thankful these were not swooping vultures or swooping pigeons. Several of the students said their biggest frustration with the owls was that they never saw them coming. Vultures and pigeons make noise in flight, but owls are silent attackers.

So it is in life. Sometimes the most devastating attack on the Christian is when we least expect it. We never see it coming. Satan ("Beowlzebub," in this case) can be extremely cunning. He knows he does not always have to confront us with the vultures of wealth, power, greed, or uncontrolled anger. He can creep up on us through pride, laziness, lack of self-control, or not spending enough time with family—like the silent attack of a supposedly innocent owl.

How do we defend ourselves from such attacks? Matthew 26:41 says, "Watch and pray so that you will not fall into temptation." While he preys on our weaknesses, we should be praying for strength. Birds of prey are no match for words of prayer, because preying claws cannot undo the grasp of praying hands.

It's a Dog-Eat-Dog World, and Cats Are Waiting Tables

I am glad my Chihuahuas cannot read, because they would have seen a *Time* magazine article about all the amenities available to today's dog—ranging from day-care centers to pet motels equipped with Barka Loungers. My Chihuahuas, Molly and Tiny, are offered the no-frills, economy plan consisting of food, water, rest-room facilities, and television.

One of today's pet luxuries is a country club where you must first bring in your dog for an interview. My dogs, who are basically field rats on a caffeine high, do poorly in interviews. I'm not saying they bounce off the baseboards (they can't reach the walls), but they could be the poster dogs for Ritalin. All they do during interviews is sniff, growl, bark, and boof. A "boof" is what happens when a small intelligence-delayed dog barks with its mouth closed, mostly just blowing out its jowls. As Will Rogers's dog said, "I never met a lawn I didn't like"—and when it comes to lawn decorations, my Chihuahuas can rumble with the big dogs.

Other advances include experimental medical treatments for dog problems. One dog's biting problem was treated with acupuncture—eight needles inserted between his neck and his hips. It cured him from biting, but now he leaks. Several drugs, including herbal medicines, are being tested as treatments for dog ailments. Even Prozac has been used to help treat obsessive or destructive behavior, constant barking, tail chasing, and aggression. Well, that's fine for Congress, but will it work on dogs?

Some dogs suffer from separation anxiety, which causes biting and clawing through walls—but then again, so does watching ice dancing on television. Knowing my dogs, they would get uppity after staying at a dog spa for two weeks and begin using police crime-scene tape to mark their territory.

When you get right down to it, most dogs have a pretty good life, mainly because they have someone to take care of them. But dogs don't have anything on us. We have the Great Shepherd, and the nonbelieving world watches to see what, if anything, is different about us because we have been with God. Life is such a treat, and anytime we fail to live it according to the grace God has given us, we ought to be scolded.

Proverbs 17:22 says, "A cheerful heart is good medicine, but a crushed spirit dries up the bones." A dog wags its tail when it is happy, but in Christianity we see much more tail dragging than we do tail wagging.

I wonder sometimes if we don't live in a Christian-eat-Christian world, and Satan is waiting tables. Are we, like man's best friend, guilty of biting the Hand that feeds us?

When Life Gives You Cicadas, Make Earrings

It is ten o'clock at night, and you have just opened the windows in your bedroom. The first warm night of spring has arrived, and you want to hear the soothing sounds of nature. Instead, what you hear is a woodpecker building a condo right outside your bedroom, your neighbor starting up his Camaro with no muffler, and what sounds like two cats attacking each other with poorly played violins. Now that you've heard nature, you close the window and go to bed.

You have just about counted your last wolverine (hey, anyone can count sheep) when you hear a loud, high-pitched, nerve-wracking, sleep-shattering, incessant shrieking. What does it mean? Well, it probably means your visiting mother-in-law was not pleased with supper, or your wife was walking through the bedroom in the dark and stepped on one of your Chihuahuas' squeaky toys. If you don't have a mother-in-law or a Chihuahua, then it means your house has been invaded by cicadas.

According to a recent newspaper article, in a Paul Revere sort of way, the cicadas are coming. A cicada, for those of you who are entomologically impaired, is an insect with a stout body, wide blunt head, and protruding eyes. Again, I realize this could be describing your mother-in-law, but we have already ruled her out. Cicadas live underground for years, come out long enough to lay a bunch of eggs, create a lot of noise for a few weeks, and then disappear. They are very similar to losing presidential candidates.

The cicadas coming here are seventeen-year cicadas. If there is anything I fear, it is teenage cicadas. No pizza will be safe. This particular group is also known as the periodical cicada, which means after it lays eggs, for seventeen years it sits around the den reading magazines. In some species, the male makes all the noise while the female, for all practical purposes, is mute. This would explain why there are no cicada hair salons.

We had an invasion of cicadas several years ago in Middle Tennessee. The noise was awful, and they left wings and body parts everywhere. Many people complained. Entomologists tell us that the noise is actually a song of courtship. In the midst of the inconvenience, one resourceful woman spent time scavenging for the wings to make cicada earrings.

As Christians, we should be the champions of making something good out of a bad situation. When we feel engulfed by the pressures of just getting by from day to day and are on the verge of giving in, our song should be "All to Jesus I Surrender."

Through His Word, God offers us a way to deal with the cicadas in life. "We know that in all things God works for the good of those who love him" (Romans 8:28) and "I can do everything with the help of Christ who gives me the strength I need" (Philippians 4:13 NLT) should be more than just favorite verses to quote on testimony night at church. They should be a way of life, our motivation for living every day to the fullest . . . and turning cicadas into earrings.

Chapter 3:

If Life Is a Bed of Roses, Then Someone Flipped My Mattress

Lessons from Day-to-Day Living

Reality's Bite Is Usually Worse Than Its Bark

Some of you won't like this statement, but it's true: I have watched most of the so-called reality television shows. The only one I like is the one where they build a house for a needy family in seven days. (To me, the phrase reality television is an oxymoron. Most of the shows remind me of only half that word.) They have titles like *Average Joe, Last Comic Standing, The Amazing Race, Who's Your Daddy?, Fear Factor, Survivor,* and *Wife Swap* (not what you think but still really strange).

Many of these shows involve prize money, and the winners are paid hundreds of thousands of dollars for being rude, malicious, mean, gross, and abusive, and for having really bad hair. Come to think of it, except for the money, that sounds like a training school for church secretaries. (Of course, I used those same character qualities to be elected president of my college fraternity.)

What is real or sensible about diving for a pig's tongue in a vat of animal fat? If I want to see that, I'll drive to a particular area in rural

Georgia and attend a wedding reception. Who cares about a group of people sitting around conniving, backbiting, yelling at each other, and deciding who they are going to vote out? Shoot, church people do that every Monday. I want to see an episode of *Wife Swap* combined with *The Simple Life,* where a man in Arkansas walks into a pawnshop and trades his wife for a good deer rifle.

Reality is the story of a giraffe that killed an American pastor at a hotel in Kenya. The pastor was trampled to death on the game preserve next to the hotel. Evidently, the giraffe had been the only member to vote against him when the pastor went to the church for a trial sermon. The rest of the congregation was ready to take a chance on the young, inexperienced preacher, but the giraffe was simply unwilling to stick his neck out.

You want reality? Why don't we see television cameras following a schoolteacher through her day or a factory worker doing his job or a farmer planting crops? Where are the cameras when a parent is up all night with a sick child or a single mother is at the end of her monthly paycheck with more bills to pay? Reality is sitting in a hospital waiting room after your mother's surgery or telling your wife you just got laid off at work.

Reality barks at us every day. Sometimes it bites. When it does, God is always there to soothe the wound. That's the "thy rod and staff, they comfort me" part of the Twenty-Third Psalm. It also says we should fear no evil because He is with us.

You want reality? We come to God as an average Joe, but He gives us an extreme makeover. The Bible tells us over and over that while we are in the real world, our heavenly Father wants to be involved in our simple life and can handle any fear factor. In the amazing race of gods, our heavenly Father would be the last God standing.

Who's *your* Daddy?

Don't Worry about Your Baggage
When You Check Out of Heartbreak Hotel

t has been twenty-six years—twenty-five of marriage and one of
engagement—since I exited the waters of the dating pool. As best
I can recall, they were treacherous waters. When I was a student
at Ouachita Baptist University, there was one female I tried to woo
on several different occasions. She always said no and became a challenge. She refused the woo. I even followed the theme of a popular
television show at the time and sent her a cassette tape that said she
would self-destruct in fifteen seconds if she turned down her mission
of going out with me. She chose the self-destruction.

For one big event on campus, I was turned down by eighteen different girls in one week. I even bathed and covered my Bubba teeth.
By the time I got to numbers eleven through eighteen, I was calling
perfect strangers out of the college directory. I finally went by myself.
I had such a great time; I asked myself out several more times dur-

ing college. I saved a lot of money and had very few rejections. But eventually I broke up with myself. We just couldn't see eye to eye on anything.

I wish I had studied the dating habits of some of the animal world for direction. There are some reptile courtships in which the males change shape and color and produce loud noises. I produced many loud noises in college, but it got me nowhere with the girls. Scientists in Central America have studied the guan, a turkeylike bird, and discovered that the female prefers a male who is relatively parasite free. Except for living in a men's dorm with a community bathroom down the hall and eating a hot-dog pizza in the cafeteria, I was relatively parasite free.

In one species of grouse, the male tries to influence the female with his dazzling dancing. My dancing was more in the befuddling mode. There is one other unique ritual. When some species of bears meet, there are sounds of squeals, bugles, groans, and growls. No, wait a minute. That was on an episode of *The Dating Game*.

In the 1950s, there was a hit song about a lonely place people go to dwell when they suffer from the pain of a broken relationship. That story dealt with a boy-girl relationship, but Heartbreak Hotel has people checking in all the time for other reasons: a friend let them down, they had a bad experience at work, a loved one died, or maybe there was a difficult family situation at home.

Checking in is easy. Just bring your baggage. We all check in to Heartbreak Hotel at one time or another, because we don't live perfect lives. Sometimes we question God, and that is OK. But we must guard against putting on the coat of pride and getting comfortable in the bed of self-pity.

We can check in by ourselves, but we need help to get out. We must have a heart-to-heart talk with the Manager and leave our baggage with Him. Baggage can be a real bear, but He can handle it all and there is no charge. It's been paid for. There is something else about this Manager. For our convenience, comfort, security, and well-being . . . He always leaves the Light on.

It's Hard to Cage a Party Animal

I love parties. My idea of the perfect party is me sitting in my recliner with a Mountain Dew, some cheese dip and chips, a John Wayne movie, and a box of dog biscuits. Those are for the dogs. They get bored with John Wayne after about two hours. If I'm living on the edge that day, I will put jalapeños in the cheese dip. Sometimes, and this is rare, when I really want to do something off the wall, I won't use the remote control. Then there are those days when I don't just throw caution to the wind; I kick it out of the house and stay up until six . . . *p.m.*

It doesn't get any better than that, unless you attend the Toad Suck Daze festival in Conway, Arkansas. Don't laugh. It was named the 1998 Festival of the Year in Arkansas. It barely beat out Name That Cousin and Carp Fest. No toads are actually harmed during the festival. It's just one of those phrases that makes your grandmother want to cringe. It also gives you a wonderful opportunity to go into any local restaurant and ask the waitress if she has frog legs; whereupon the answer is usually, "No, I've always walked like that."

Another fun party is the Great Wisconsin Cheese Festival. One of the most fun competitions—and another phrase that messes with your grandmother's mind—is the Cheese Curd Eating Contest. Curd comes from sour milk and gives us such wonderful cheeses as Limburger (named after a really smelly 1920s pilot) and Gorgonzola (named after the 1950s monster who ate Tokyo).

Wisconsin has nothing on a town in Gloucester, England. Cooper's Hill hosts the annual Cheese Rolling Festival. It involves chasing a seven-pound block of Double Gloucester cheese down a three-hundred-yard hill. The winner gets to slice the cheese. Innocent bystanders can get wounded by errant cheese. One person was hit in the head by a cheese clump and had to be taken to the doctor. It knocked him silly for a while. He thought he had seen the Loch Ness Muenster.

These are great celebrations, but there is more than one way to spell *celebrate*. Not everyone parties, but we all should. Some people *cell-ebrate* life because they live their lives imprisoned by something—drugs, alcohol, work, or self-doubt. Others *sell-ebrate* life because they are motivated by money, power, success, and staying ahead of the other guy.

Do you cringe when you see the way some people live? Does it seem as though they are spending their lives chasing a cheese log down a hill? Jesus said, "I have come that they may have life, and that they may have it more abundantly" (John 10:10 NKJV).

Do you know someone who is *cell-ebrating* life because they are imprisoned by something? You need to introduce them to the One who can pardon them. Do you know someone who *sell-ebrates* life by stepping on others while climbing the ladder of success? You need to introduce them to the One who gave His life and climbed a hill called Mount Calvary.

Tell them about the abundant life. Invite them to the party. Accepting the invitation is the only way to truly live in celebration because you know the One who threw the party.

Playing from the Hazard Is Par for the Course

As the flowers begin lifting their warbles in song, as the robins begin wearing short-sleeved shirts, and as the car salesmen begin bursting out all over, causing everyone to sneeze—it can only mean one thing . . . you probably live in California. It could also mean spring is just around the corner.

Like Sears returning to Roebuck, like the condos returning to the land of Minium, and like the geographically impaired swallows returning to Chattanooga, I shall in*stink*ively (emphasis on the "stink") return to the golf course. I am as natural on a golf course as hair on bacon. My swing is to golf what Ernest T. Bass is to opera. When I play, local residents board up their windows, squirrels wear helmets, and carp hide their young. I am so scary on the golf course that even death takes a holiday.

My PGA (Pathetic Golf Association) equipment consists of clubs, balls, tees, weed whacker, backhoe for replacing divots, gopher repair kit, a tree identification chart, and a CB radio. My CB handle is Red Riding Hood, because I normally play over the river and through the woods. I play not only across fairways but also across subdivisions. Concerned and sometimes horrified golfers do not yell out the gentlemanly "Fore!" They follow the path of my ball and scream out the appropriate neighborhood.

Sometimes my shots are mysteriously attracted to obstacles known as "hazards." These hazards have a tendency to make it extremely difficult to enjoy a relaxing and profanity-free round of golf. They can consist of sand traps, trees, oceans, herds of bison, New Jersey, a 1964 Rambler, unsuspecting wives who think you are in a business meeting, and one stunned fellow in Bermuda shorts and black socks. I didn't think I would hit him because he was standing behind me.

The unique thing about golf is that if you land in a hazard, there is no penalty! Can you believe it? You just place your ball out in the open on some low-cut grass, called a "fairway," which offers an easier shot.

One of the determining factors in our enjoyment of golf is how we react to landing in one of the hazards. Even the pros land in hazards. The difference is they know how to get out. It is the same in life. God never promised us a hazard-free round of living but He does offer a fair way, paved with mercy and grace, for everyone to play through. It is called trust.

Nahum 1:7 says, "The LORD is good, a refuge in times of trouble. He cares for those who trust in him." We cannot allow ourselves to be trapped by circumstances in our drive to play the course in life which God has designed. They can be both frustrating in our enjoyment of the Game and hazardous to our spiritual health.

If we land in a hazard, we need to get a firm grip on God's Word and take another shot. If we put our trust in the Instructor, we will have a much more pleasing scorecard to share when we reach the Clubhouse.

Real Christianity Seldom Has an Audience, but Reel Christianity Always Does

I love watching movies. Nothing beats the sensation when you get up out of your seat and your feet make a giant "sucking" noise because of the three-inch layer of spilled soft drinks, melted twelve-dollar chocolate bars, and dead gummy bears . . . and that's just in my den. It is much worse at the theater. I did not choose to watch much of the recent Academy Awards show, but I did read a few descriptions of the clothing—or lack thereof. One evening gown was described as "a strapless Carolina Herrera gown" and another as "a yellow-belted Valentino."

Just once I want to hear something like this:

OVERDRAMATIC FASHION COMMENTATOR: "Oh, that is gorgeous. She is wearing a Guy Laroche pewter gown with matching tulle trim."

BUBBA: "Uh, no, that there looks more like an exploding tackle box from Bill Dance Outdoors."

OVERDRAMATIC FASHION COMMENTATOR: "Ooh! That is a Versace shoulder-grazing black gown."

BUBBA: "I don't know what a shoulder-grazing gown is, but on her I think it answers the question, 'Where's the beef?'"

I have found a list of movies that never made it to the public. There was a movie about fictional firemen in Middle Earth who climbed ladders and put out fires by spraying them with waterlogged hobbits. It was called *Lord of the Rungs*. Charlton Heston reprised his role as Moses in *Moles in the Floor of Heaven*, where Moses was recalled to active duty to deal with an eleventh plague.

The tearjerker of the year would have been *Mr. Holland's Porpoise*. A middle-aged music teacher, thinking his life is a waste, threw caution to the wind. The wind threw it back, and Mr. Holland taught his porpoise how to play the piano. The porpoise then ran away to the Ivory Coast and conveniently married a piano tuna.

Movies are great fun, as long as we remember never to confuse the *reel* world with the *real* world. When I was younger, I had to be reminded during particularly scary scenes that it was only a movie. The people on the screen were only playing a role. They were not really in danger. They were actors—people acting like somebody else.

Maybe there is more similarity between *real* life and *reel* life than we would like to think. Christians always have an audience. We often are guilty of saying one thing with our mouth but doing the opposite with our life. People notice, and we must ask ourselves a question. Are we living in the real world and being genuine Christians, or are we just existing in the reel world . . . and only playing a role?

People are watching us. To put it in movie terms, if our actions are full of *Pride and Prejudice*, then our words will be *Gone with the Wind*.

lesson 26

Confession Is Good for the Sale

There are several events in a marriage that have the potential of becoming battlegrounds. One is moving the remote control from its assigned position next to the recliner. A second one is not using enough superlatives to describe your wife's new hairstyle. The third one is having a garage sale. As far as I know, the remote is next to the recliner, and after Beverly's last salon visit I used twenty-three supererogatory adjectives to describe her supercilious and yet superfluous new look. That can only mean we had a garage sale recently.

The first garage sale occurred in 1624 in what is now New York City. The Manhattan Indians needed money. The conversation in the mud hut went like this:

FIRST INDIAN: "We must have money. Without it, we cannot move our baseball team to Cleveland."

SECOND INDIAN: "I know! Let's have a garage sale!"

THIRD INDIAN: "What's a garage?"

HOME PLATE INDIAN: "I can't tell you that."

SHORTSTOP INDIAN: "You can tell me. I'm a doctor."

Well, this inane conversation went on and on until they ultimately invented the garage sale. They got together some things they no longer needed: beads, used deerskins, a canoe with a hole in the bottom, and Manhattan Island. The beads, skins, and canoe brought in $75,000. The island went for $24 . . . marked down from $100.

In our personal garage sale we had no such luxurious items, although we did put a price tag on one of our Chihuahuas for about an hour. We also sold a brass squirrel that was old, run-down, and so melted from years in the sun it had been transformed from the likeness of an innocent squirrel leisurely eating an acorn to the image of a maniacal squirrel frantically picking his nose.

We had the standard garage sale fodder, such as a flowering onion maker, a yellow ceramic flying horse with pink wings, an eight-by-ten-inch glossy of me, and a bookend. The most unusual item we had was a massage mat, also known as a body revitalizer. My physical journey has taken me beyond the realm of revitalization, so I sold it to a woman with three preschoolers. The entire ordeal reminded me of an old American axiom: "Today's Christmas could be tomorrow's garage sale."

We all need to clean out our house and garage now and then, even if we don't have a garage sale. The same could be said for our spiritual house. We must go through our hearts and minds and clear out everything we don't need. We need a spiritual cleaning. It's called confession, and it revitalizes our soul.

It's during confession we get rid of negative thoughts, bad attitudes, and other sins we try not to think about. First John 1:9

says, "If we confess our sins, He is faithful and righteous to forgive us our sins and to cleanse us from all unrighteousness" (NASB).

Garage sales clear out your house and give you more room to live. Confession is a fresh wind that clears out your heart and gives God more room to live in you.

God Holds the Line
When a Christian Gets Lost in Space

I t is the most excruciatingly painful and monstrously horrifying experience I have had on an annual basis, with the exception of cleaning my Chihuahuas and getting a haircut. On a terror scale of one to ten, this ranks just above programming my VCR and watching my daughter turn thirteen. It is an annual rite of passage involving millions of bewildered parents all over the known United States and Texas.

It is more stressful than shopping for the newest toy at Christmas, and it takes more patience than watching your in-laws let your child do something you told them never to do . . . and your in-laws know you told them never to do it. This makes the Running of the Bulls look like a duck walk on a Sunday afternoon in the park. It is so evil scientists just refer to it as "SSSSSSSSS" (the symbol of the snake)—the "Sickeningly Squeamish, Shock-

ingly Shameless, Saturday School-Supply Shopping Stampede."
In other words, it's time to shop for school supplies.

Through my own shallow study and observation, I have decided
it is more complicated, expensive, and time consuming to buy the
correct school supplies than it is to purchase a foreign country. If
you don't have the right supplies, your child gets ostrich eyes . . . or is
it ostracized? Something needs to change. When we became parents, we were not told that diapers have a load limit and we were
definitely not warned about shopping for school supplies.

I haven't seen that much violence since I tried to organize an
Eat the Whale rally. Someone needs to offer a modified Lamaze
class for parents who expect to shop for school supplies the natural
way, with just a coach, a tennis ball, no epidural, and some timely
bad language. We could practice whistling, breathing, screaming,
and placing the tennis ball at the pressure point causing the most
pain and stress. In my shopping excursion, it would have been in
the mouths of a woman in her midthirties and her two children,
Banshee and Tasmanian Devil.

You need to go shopping for school supplies just to see the millions of varieties of pens now available. There is even one pen with
a built-in antibacterial agent that actually fights bacteria. I don't
really care about that. I just want a pen that writes without skip-
ping, because the basic purpose of a pen is to write solid lines.

Like the pen that skips, when we stray from our basic purpose
as Christians—to love God and love our neighbor—we sometimes live our lives with too many spaces in the solid lines. Our
solid lines may include prayer and reading the Bible. The question
is, what are we doing in the spaces? First John 3:18 says, "My children, our love should not be just words and talk; it must be true
love, which shows itself in action" (TEV).

Are we visiting people in the nursing homes? Are we volunteering at a food bank or offering aid at a homeless shelter? We will never write a perfectly solid line. Only Jesus did. But we can fill our spaces by trying to live every moment to please God. In that sense, it's not so bad to be lost in space.

Don't Leave the Ground
if Your Control Tower Is Vacant

everal years ago, when I was a youth minister and had spack-ling compound for brains, I took my youth group to Panama City Beach, Florida, for a spring break camp. I must be ex-aggeratingly honest with you. It was beyond scary. It was like a nightmare out of *The Bare Witch Project*. (This was a little-known documentary film in the '70s about three young filmmakers who mysteriously disappeared at a nudist colony in Maryland while searching for a woman known only as Endora.)

It was like being on a deserted island with nothing but a ste-reo . . . and the only records were polka music. It was the most terrifying, ghastly, stomach-churning, bone-breaking, patience-destroying experience of my entire hair-impaired and pizza-inten-sive youth ministry. But when we finished loading the trailer and got rid of the parents, everything was fine.

Taking a bus ride with teenagers has all the thrill and adventure of performing a self-appendectomy. School is always in session, and the hot topics of discussion are: sociology ("He took my CD player!"), geography ("Are we there yet?"), biology ("I have to go to the bathroom!"), and math ("How long before we get there?"). The same teenager who can manipulate a computer keyboard like Chopin on a piano cannot grasp the concept that the more liquid you drink, the more stops the bus has to make.

Neither can he read highway signs that might actually tell him what state he is in, usually confusion. During the week we went to a store called Alvin's Island, where these same computer-literate teenagers spent thousands of dollars on future garage-sale items like shark back scratchers and octopus-under-glass paperweights. With all the cheap souvenirs, gaudy hats, ugly mugs, and live sharks, it looked like your average national political convention.

While walking on the beach one day, I noticed some little white birds, about the size of robins on steroids, trying to fly against the wind. It looked almost like they were stopped in midflight, but their wings were constantly moving. They would fly for a while, stop and rest, and then try again. Not once did I see one turn back and go the other direction. They kept going.

I wish we could do as well in our walk with God. God never promised us a wind-aided life. Sometimes, in order for us to get to where God wants us to be, we, too, must fly against the wind—when it would be so much easier to simply go with the flow. We will have trials, but like the birds, we must keep going forward and not turn back.

Hebrews 12:1 says, "Let us run with endurance the race that God has set before us" (NLT). No matter how difficult the flight becomes, God still controls the wind. The only question is, does God control us?

You Can't Set an Alarm with Father Time

Several alarming incidents in recent days have caused me to realize I may be approaching middle age, in the same sense the *Titanic* may have approached an iceberg. It all started when my son bought a new pair of jeans. Both cuffs were ripped. Apparently they come that way now. He was proud. I thought he should have gotten a discount.

At least his jeans went all the way above his knees. There is a trend toward pants called "low-rise." Isn't that an oxymoron? They seem to be lowering more than they are rising. Bending over gracefully becomes a challenge, and you can quickly see how the designers have brought one era of fashion to an abrupt end.

My other sartorially challenging incident can only be described as the Hindenburg of fashion emergencies. I went out to retrieve the morning paper wearing a red tank top, orange shorts, black socks, and brown loafers . . . and I didn't care. That is disturbing.

Thank goodness my daughter didn't see me. Dressing like that is just one John Deere tractor cap and a pair of denim overalls away from playing checkers in front of the general store or being a senior adult tourist on the beach in Destin.

Clothing is only one area where I feel the pain of Father Time punishing me. Things that used to be funny are now irritating, like the nauseating commercial about removing unsightly hair. Five women are sitting in a den laughing. One of them has a hairy leg. She has let the hair grow out in order to test a new hair removal spray. Two hard questions need to be asked. Who let the women out of the kitchen? And why would that woman walk around in public with only one hairy leg?

Motion-sensitive ceramic frogs used to be funny, in that fingernails-on-the-blackboard sort of way. Then came a largemouth bass singing "Don't worry, be happy." With the exception of a piano, I am not one who can be influenced emotionally by anything with scales. I don't want a dead fish singing at me or telling me to be happy when I walk into a store and see the price tag on a croaking frog.

The final arena where age has trampled ability is my golf game. I played a few weeks ago and watched my friend's drives explode off the tee box as if they were shot from a howitzer. My drives sauntered aimlessly off the tee like water dribbling out of an almost-empty water gun. Each drive took a casual stroll in the woods or a quick dip in the pond, never to be seen again.

Being born in 1952 puts me almost dead center of the generation called baby boomers. It seems there are more days when my boom is closer to a fizzle. I don't know what "old" is. When I was twenty, I thought twenty-seven was old. Now I have jeans that old. I've enjoyed every age I've been so far, and I would certainly not go back. I am happy where I am.

Psalm 39:5 tells us that God made our days "as a mere handbreadth" and our lifetime "as nothing." In other words, age does not matter to God. Just because we are getting older does not mean we cannot serve God gracefully and continue to be imitators of Christ. We do that at whatever age we find ourselves.

Age does not matter. But it does matter what we do with the "Rock of all ages."

Looking at Life through Ripped Shorts and Changing Perspectives

I t is interesting to note how counties welcome motorists into their community with a descriptive sign. I saw one sign recently that read, "Welcome to So-and-So County, home of the finest people in the world." How do they know that? Did someone do a survey? Did they narrow the choices by playing Survivor? Where does that leave the rest of us? One store in this fine county had a sign advertising furniture. The "n" in "furniture" was backward. I guess their spelling skills were not so fine.

I stopped at a fine mom-and-pop greasy hamburger joint. I do that a lot on the road, because I tire easily of the fast-food restaurant ceiling-tile hamburgers. I ordered a double cheeseburger with extra cheese and a large chocolate shake. I try to watch my cholesterol, so I did not order fries. I took one bite of that fine cheeseburger and threw it into one of their fine trash cans. It was fine, if you don't mind meat of questionable pedigree. It probably depends on how you look at it.

I went to my thirty-year high-school reunion at Hall High School in Little Rock, Arkansas, in July 2000. I got to roam the same halls I had roamed thirty years earlier. Only the echo was different. Typical of my life and personality, halfway through the tour I discovered something every male has to face at least once in front of people: a rip in the shorts. It was in a location where rips always seem to go. It is their vacation getaway, a Club Med for rips, and I was wearing dark walking shorts.

The good news was that the rip was only visible when I sat down. Every real man knows there is no manly way to sit with ripped shorts. So I stood a lot. In 1970, ripped shorts would have sent me into a maniacal hoedown of panic, stress, and terminal embarrassment. In 2000, having survived teenagers and hundreds of Keystone Cops–like church business meetings, dealing with ripped shorts was a walk in the park. It's all a matter of perspective.

How do you look at life? Do you wake up every day thanking God for another day of life and all of the blessings He has given, or do you lie awake at night thinking of different ways to find fault with others? When rain comes, do you complain about lost opportunities outdoors, or do you think of the good it brings and anticipate the rainbow? When the farmer looks at rain, he sees life. It's all a matter of perspective.

God changes us in many ways when we become His children. He also changes our perspective. If we are to be who He wants us to be, we must learn to look at life through God-colored glasses. It will change the way we look at others. It's all a matter of perspective. You see, perspective is a God thing . . . and what really matters in life is what God thinks of us.

Chapter 4:

Does History Repeat Itself Because Nobody Listened the First Time?

Lessons from History about His Story

God Is Our Refuge and Strength,
but He Is Also a God of Constant Sorrows

Johnstown, Pennsylvania, was once devastated by a flood. The town was built on a flood plain at the fork of two rivers. Several miles up one of the rivers was a lake, the water held back by a poorly maintained dam. It was a standing joke every spring that the dam might not hold.

The dam broke on May 31, 1889, sending twenty million tons of water down the valley. More than twenty-two hundred people died, with more left homeless. Bodies were found as far away as Cincinnati and as late as 1911. At that time, it was the worst flood in our nation's history. Fingers of blame were pointed at individuals. It was five years before Johnstown fully recovered.

In April 1906, California was rocked by one of the most significant earthquakes of all time. It hit San Francisco the hardest. The population at the time was 400,000. Three thousand people died;

lesson 31

225,000 were left homeless. The earthquake sparked a fire that caused even more damage. It burned more than 28,000 buildings along a stretch of 490 city blocks.

The quake was felt all the way to Oregon and into central Nevada. It was devastating. Naturally, people sought to lay blame. An eyewitness reported seeing a man standing in the street yelling, "The Lord did it!" It took years, but San Francisco recovered.

On the morning of August 29, 2005, Hurricane Katrina decimated the Gulf Coast from Mobile, Alabama, to New Orleans, Louisiana. It was the most expensive hurricane ever to hit the United States. Places like Biloxi, Gulfport, and Pass Christian in Mississippi were devastated. The storm damaged cities all the way to Jackson, Mississippi. Because of the levee failures, 80 percent of New Orleans was flooded. The cleanup is going to be a lengthy process. It will take months and years, but the people will return. They have to. It is their home. It is our home. It is part of America.

Fingers of blame have again been pointed. Some doomsday preachers have jumped on the God bandwagon by saying it is His retribution for our nation's sin. They seem to take particular interest in catastrophes to see how they fit into their end-of-the-world scheme. We live in a fallen world. Devastation and catastrophe have been around for a long time and will be here until God decides differently.

This is not a time to point fingers. Democrats died. Republicans died. Christians died. Non-Christians died. African-Americans died. Anglo-Americans died. Asian-Americans died. Hispanic-Americans died. People cried. God cried. It is time for all of us to pull together, especially churches. It is time to help and time to pray. It is time to turn to our fellow Americans for help and to our God for strength.

There is power in the storms of nature. There is more power in the God of nature. Rest assured, as we work side by side with those in need, the sweat of man will mingle with the tears of God. The problem with mixing God and catastrophes is that when God cries, no one is around to see the tears.

Lesson 32

*If at First You Don't Succeed,
Don't Tell Your Mother-in-Law*

There have been many inventions in the last two hundred years that define Americans as what we are today . . . mostly spoiled, whiny brats. Some favorites on the list are the cotton gin, invisible tape (so named because we never can find it when it we need it), gun racks, spray butter, cars in the driveway on concrete blocks, portable outhouses, automobiles the size of train engines, fake deer on the front lawn, and a nose-hair trimmer. Numbers one and two on the list are soybean burgers and burping Tupperware lids. Of course, I'm kidding. Everyone knows we could not do without electricity, telephones, and the flushable vehicle spittoon.

Without electricity, there would be no stereos, video games, or televisions, and we would have to actually communicate with our children. Without telephones, we would have no way to call in late for work, and the only way to spread gossip would be face to face.

The flushable vehicle spittoon was invented so southern grandmothers would have someplace to spit while they are driving. This replaces the original design of a plastic cup with a paper towel in the bottom. My only requirement for spitting and driving is that the window be down.

We have Thomas Edison to thank for inventing the electric light bulb. Of course, nobody remembers that Edison failed many times before he came up with the right combination of parts and gizmos to perfect the light bulb. It took ten thousand different failed experiments before he found success. He couldn't figure out why the bulb would not stay on for very long. He eventually discovered his teenage daughter never turned the light off when she left the room.

Alexander Graham Bell went through many failed experiments before he invented the telephone. Everyone knows the conversation that ensued on that historic day. Bell: "Watson, come here. I need you!" Watson: "If you'd like to make a call, please hang up and dial the operator."

Success is wonderful and reassuring, but besides death and taxes, each of us is also going to face failure at some point in our lives. How did you manage failure in the past? Are you better prepared to deal with it in the present? Your daughter fails to make the cheerleading squad, or your son fails to make all-state band. You fail to get that promotion at work you thought you deserved.

We learn from characters in the Bible that we can't let failure keep us down. David failed God in the Old Testament. He came back. Paul started out as a persecutor of Christians. He came back as a defender of the faith. Paul says, "The one thing I do, however, is to forget what is behind me and do my best to reach what is ahead" (Philippians 3:13 TEV).

Make your failures building blocks, not stumbling blocks. If Edison had stopped after his first failure, we may never have seen artificial light. If God had stopped with His failure in Adam and Eve, we never would have seen Jesus, the true Light of the world.

Hysterical Trip on a Historical Trail Leads to a Heavenly Truth

In June 1997, I took my first trip with the senior adults of Springfield Baptist Church. (At that time, they innocently called themselves the LLL Club. During the trip I discovered it meant Laughter, Leave, and Leftover—Laughter, because there was a lot of it; Leave, as in "taken leave of their senses"; and Leftover, as in "whenever we ate, there was nothing left over.") We loaded the bus (the only way we could get the bus to agree to go was to get it loaded) and headed for Natchez, Mississippi, along the Natchez Trace.

The Natchez Trace was named after Irving Natchez, an eighteenth-century artist who bought every piece of tracing paper at Wal-Mart and traced a line from Natchez to Nashville. It was the main trade route connecting those two cities from 1785 to 1820. They had to build another road when the tracing paper finally eroded into the ground. On the Trace, there are points of historical significance where you can stop and read interesting facts, study ancient burial grounds, and when no one is looking, steal historical plums off of the historical trees.

Entering Natchez was like stepping back in time, or stepping on to our bus full of senior adults. Natchez has the largest collection of antebellum homes in the South. *Antebellum*, of course, is a Latin word meaning "large cruise ship–size houses built by extremely rich people before the Civil War." *Ante* really means "before," so to be technically correct we must say that these houses were built before the bellum.

We even had the age authenticated by several people in our group who were actually in Natchez in 1860. As we took tours of the homes, our guides described the elaborate furnishings and table settings with classy words like *Queen Anne, King George, Louis XIV,* and *Victorian.* It was very similar to the way tour guides will describe my house in 150 years. They will use classy terms like *Early Garage Sale, Flea Market, Vinyl City, Tupperware, Sofa with Broken Leg,* and *Dog Infused.*

The most beautiful place we saw was a house called Longwood, a six-story home built in 1860. It had one small problem: only the outside and the basement were finished. Floors two through six were only a shell, including the scaffolding used during construction. When the Civil War began, the workers dropped what they were doing and went home, leaving the house with a misleadingly gorgeous exterior and an unfinished interior.

I had never seen a house like that before, but we all have seen people whose spiritual house is in similar disarray. They look fine on the outside, but the inside is only a shell. They are spiritually hollow. They may never have been introduced to the Master

Builder who could show them how to do the inside work necessary for a complete and lasting house. Or they could be Christians who have never allowed the Master Carpenter to do His finishing work in them. "And I am sure that God, who began the good work within you, will continue his work until it is finally finished on that day when Christ Jesus comes back again" (Philippians 1:6 NLT).

Like Longwood, these "houses" will always be nice attractions, but until they are finished they will never fulfill the original intent of the Designer.

Soaring with the Eagles or Souring with the Turkeys?

had the opportunity several years ago to travel to Reelfoot Lake in West Tennessee to observe our country's storied national emblem, the bald senior adult. I watched them for hours during a feeding frenzy in their natural habitat—the cafeteria. When the carnage was over, I turned my attention to the bald eagle, the other national emblem.

Very much like senior adults, the bald eagle is seasonal and migrates to where the food is. While migrating, they ride columns of rising air and can average about thirty miles per hour. Baby eagles are called eaglets, or chicks. Most breeding and hatching is done in the north, but occasionally there are some eaglets born in the southernmost part of the United States. These, of course, would be the Dixie chicks.

The bald eagle was actually the third emblem choice of our forefathers. Their first choice was the cow. With its calm appearance and leisurely gait, the cow inspired a bucolic picture of America. Our forefathers soon discovered it also inspired really good hamburgers. They were looking for something more flight-capable and realized that except for tornado movies and too much caffeine, cows very seldom fly . . . although they have been known to occasionally see a high diddle diddle and jump over the moon.

As a second choice, in a charge led by Ben Franklin, they elected the turkey . . . um, the bird, not John Adams. However, there were some drawbacks. The turkey was slow and awkward. Rather than being prone to flight, it was rather flighty. This was a perfect symbol for the eventual capital of Washington, D.C., but the turkey's only flying experience was limited to one episode of *WKRP in Cincinnati.* Our founding fathers opted for the bald eagle, so named because they failed to use Rogaine . . . um, the eagles, not our forefathers. They wore Whigs.

Eagles are also mentioned in the Old Testament. The prophet Micah says to "make yourselves as bald as the eagle" (1:16 NRSV). I've mastered that. Isaiah wrote, "Those who wait for the LORD shall renew their strength, they shall mount up with wings like eagles, they shall run and not be weary" (40:31 NRSV). I'm still working on that.

We may pattern our lives after any number of people, but God is the One who renews our strength and lifts us up when we are weary. His wingspread is incomparable, His wisdom is infinite, and His words are indisputable. One of the problems we face today is that churches seem to have an overabundance of turkeys waiting to gobble and not enough eagles ready to soar.

Is it any wonder there is a hunting season for turkeys and not eagles? God is ready to lift us up, but if we are going to soar with the eagle, we can't take flying lessons from a turkey.

I Remember Amerigo Vespoochy, but Did Columbus Really Discover Tulsa?

In the midst of your pre-Christmas frenzy, be careful you do not miss an underrated holiday in the life of our relatively young country—Columbus Day, in October. It is in honor of Christopher Columbus and his little brother Bubba, who discovered the Southern United States in 1492.

You will remember from history that Columbus was an Italian explorer from Genoa, so named after the Italian translation of the story of Genoa and the ark. He was lounging around Spain one day with nothing to do, so he decided to discover Asia. What historians don't tell us is that Columbus's dog, Amerigo Vespoochy, spotted the first dogwoods on land. (He was going to stripe them, but after careful consideration decided on spotting.) He was never credited with the discovery because Chris just assumed he was barking up the wrong tree.

History is a little fuzzy as to why Columbus sailed west instead of actually sailing toward Asia. Two theories are prominent. One states that the eastern route was no good because most explorers of that day preferred to sail on water, and at that time no body of water could get past the Great Wall of CorningWare. Years later, when that country became more financially stable, they upgraded it to the Great Wall of China. The other theory reminds us that all shipping traffic in those years had to pass through the Atlantic, a Latin word from which we get our word *Atlanta*.

No matter which theory you accept, there are several points on which we can agree. In 1492, Columbus set sail in the wrong direction with three ships, the *Niña*, the *Pinta*, and the *Santa Maria*. Their English names were the *Shadraft*, the *Meshark*, and the *Aboatwego*, again taken from the Italian translation of the Bible. Several months later Columbus landed somewhere near Tulsa, met some hostile Indians, discovered John Wayne, and claimed the New World for Spain.

We meet people every day who are searching for something different, a new life. Like a misguided ship, they are going in the wrong direction. They may begin their journey as if they know what they are looking for, but they take too many wrong turns and look in all the wrong places. As Christians, we have a responsibility to guide them. With God's help, we can help them set their sails.

At the point of salvation, we stake our claim to a new world of faith, hope, and love; but as we continue to grow in Christ, we discover new world truths that help us mature spiritually as we live on the old. We learn what faith, hope, and love mean, and in the process we rediscover God's presence in our lives every day.

For each one of us, the journey must begin at Calvary, because until we have met Jesus at the Cross, we, like Columbus's dog, are simply barking up the wrong tree.

UNCHARTED
TERRITORY
NEXT 2000 MI
←

The Church Is in the Business of Expanding Its Boarders

In school, I always did better in English than science. I could spell *sentapeade* but did not know how many feet it had . . . other than one for each leg. I did better in history than math. I knew what the War of 1812 was, but I wasn't sure when it was fought. Several wars left me confused about who actually participated. One was the conflict called the French and Indian War. Another was the War of the Roses—a war actually fought between the Petunias and the Geraniums.

The French and Indian War pitted the Colonists, the British, and the Washington Redskins against the French and the Cleveland Indians. We won, in spite of being on the same side as soldiers in kilts. With her defeat (too much Cajun cooking), France gave the Louisiana Territory to Spain, who eventually gave it to Napoleon, a three-flavored ice cream.

36. The Church Is in the Business of Expanding Its Boarders

In 1803, our country was seventeen years old. Being a typical teen-ager, she was prone to violent mood swings, extreme growth spurts, and not being able to keep a dollar in her pocket. President Jefferson, whose theme song was "Movin' on up . . . to the East Side," wanted to buy the Louisiana Territory—which at that time consisted mostly of trees, swamps, cayenne pepper, and Huey P. Long.

James Monroe, fresh from inventing the shock absorber, bartered with France and got the land for fifteen million dollars. He then or-ganized an expedition and appointed Harry Sears and Bill Roebuck to lead it. However, they quit somewhere in Nebraska to build a gen-eral store, so history only records the exploits of their understudies, Meriwether Lewis and William Clark. Because the purchase included Texas, Oklahoma, and Kansas, historians would later refer to this rapid period of growth in the United States as Manifest Dustiny.

Every church has people who are embarking on a new jour-ney, whether it is a job change, a move from one city to another, a move to a nursing home, or even a change in marital status. They are headed for uncharted territory. They are scared. They are hurting. They are lonely. Do you have any friends who fit these categories? Give them a call or send them a note.

Two thousand years ago, the church embarked on a journey. Its destiny, manifested by God, was to expand its witness. Occa-sionally we take a wrong turn and try to expand our roles without expanding our reach. Bigger is not synonymous with better, espe-cially if our reach does not include everyone around us—regard-less of race, social status, or any other barrier we might create.

If we are going to be the church God wants us to be, we must not only minister to our own members, but we must reach out to people outside our church. Our borders will always be limitless . . . and so will our boarders.

Did the Pilgrims Drive a Mayflower Subcompact?

september 6, 1620, is an important date for turkey-loving people everywhere, because that is the date Dick Clark began broadcasting *American Bandstand.* More importantly, it was the date the Pilgrims set sail for the New World on a ship called the *Mayflower,* which sailed one month later than the seldom-mentioned and leaky *Aprilshower.*

You remember from history that the Pilgrims left their native England because of religious persecution and wild soccer riots. (This is where our contemporary phrase "soccer mom" originated.) One group, from the village of Scrooby, in Nottinghamshire, even wrote a song about their adventures. It was called "Scrooby Doo, Where Are You?" To avoid further persecution, the Pilgrims headed for America, where they could persecute the Indians. On the voyage over, like normal religious people, they began to squabble. Upon landing at Plymouth (they tried landing at Chevrolet, but it was too expensive), they formed an agreement called the Mayflower Compact. Like normal religious people, they had to create an amendment, which was called the Mayflower Subcompact. It worked out better for everyone because the weekly rates were cheaper.

The Pilgrims would not have survived that first winter without the help of an Indian named Squanto, which is also the sound a chicken makes if you drop it from the top of a three-story college dormitory. Squanto, by having a name that sounds like an aerobics exercise, quickly became fodder for a lot of Pilgrim humor. He ignored them and showed them how to plant corn, tap maple trees for syrup, and tear off the inside seal before using the squeeze ketchup bottle. On that first Thanksgiving, they feasted on corn, fruits, vegetables, and a turkey dinner from Luby's cafeteria.

Whatever the true situation was with the Indians, the Pilgrims were extremely thankful to have made it through that first New England winter. A few foul words from the Pilgrims to the Indians, and this celebration could have gone from festival to fistfull very quickly. It did not. It was such an important time that it evolved into an annual event, established by President Abraham Lincoln.

Unfortunately, the Thanksgiving holiday today is often more stressful than thankful. It was never meant to be that way. Is there tension when your family and friends gather for the Thanksgiving meal? If we truly understand the concept of living by grace, we will get beyond our differences with friends and family members and become people of Thanksgiving. Otherwise, a good idea has become just another turkey.

TECUMSEH

You Don't Have to Be Scared to Be Petrified

William Tecumseh Sherman is best known for two things in American history. Of all the Civil War generals, he had the middle name that sounded most like a sneeze. Then in November 1864, he became extremely frustrated because the Braves did not make the World Series. In the ultimate fan reaction, he burned Atlanta to the ground. This miffed the locals because it did nothing to ease the traffic problems.

There is a little-known historic side note to this episode. During Reconstruction, Scarlett O'Hara approached Ted Turner about providing money for rebuilding Atlanta. His famous answer, "Frankly, my dear, I don't give a dime," was recorded in Margaret Mitchell's recently discovered saga of preachers during the Civil War, *Gone with the Windy.*

What Sherman is not known for happened in 1878. He had

two petrified logs sent from Arizona to the Barney Fife–endorsed "Smith Brothers Institute" in Washington. The logs apparently came from an ancient conifer, which is also an expression I used to describe my fourth-grade teacher. I do not understand how a tree becomes petrified, but it involves looking into the mirror in the morning when it first wakes up.

Actually, several years ago a volcano blew up. Similar to a baby eating peas, it spewed Arizona with lava, an ancient word meaning "really hot goo." The lava felled the trees, sealing them through a process known as crystallization—a Latin word meaning, "Why don't babies like peas?" This protected the wood from the harmful effects of erosion, bacteria, and congressional speeches, but not from first-grade field trips.

It seems petrification is not limited to trees. It happens to humans too. It doesn't take much effort to become a fossil before one's time. Just sit back and watch your friends, coworkers, or neighbors erupt in a volcano of pain, suffering, or loneliness, and then do nothing. Let nature takes its course, and after years of buildup the heart becomes so hardened to those in need it will be impervious to their cry for help. Are you willing to change?

A petrified human, like a petrified tree, is impenetrable except for something sharp. With a tree, it is a chain saw. With a human, it is the Word of God that cuts through a hardened heart like a knife through air. Hebrews 4:12 says, "The word of God is alive and active, sharper than any double-edged sword. It cuts all the way through, to where soul and spirit meet, to where joints and marrow come together. It judges the desires and thoughts of the heart" (TEV).

Scripture can bring a lost person to his knees and a Christian to his senses, from fossilized to energized in one quick blow. It also changes one from being spiritually paralyzed, polarized, politicized, and pacified. Read it. Live it. And from one old fossil to another . . . let your love flow.

God Has Overcome the World, but I Still Have a Bad Knee

It was September 13, 1814. We were in the third year of the War of 1812. It was kind of like Vietnam. The British began shelling Fort McHenry in Baltimore, Maryland. An American lawyer, Francis Scott Key, was on one of the British ships. When he awoke on the morning of September 14, he noticed the American flag over Fort McHenry was still waving. That's when he penned the words to our national anthem, the theme from *Monday Night Football.* Just kidding. We all know our national anthem is "I Wish I Were an Oscar Mayer Wiener." If you have ever tried to sing the "Star-Spangled Banner," you know that Mr. Key was obviously in a lot of pain when he wrote it.

On September 13, 1847, General Winfield Scott was in command of the American army when they stormed Chapultepec in the last great battle of the Mexican-American War. The American army was outnumbered, but the Mexican army had inferior weapons. The cannon balls ended up rolling on the ground at the Americans. Not a bad way to fight a war—rolling cannon balls at each other. Each country would elect a bowling team with a leader named Earl. The shirts alone would send terror through the countryside . . . and don't forget the psychological damage done by wearing rented shoes.

As a result of losing this battle, Mexico ceded the Territory of New Mexico to the United States. At that time it included not only parts of New Mexico, Colorado, Wyoming, and Arizona, but also all of Nevada, Utah, and California. We have tried several times but have been unsuccessful in giving California back to Mexico.

It is September 13, 2005. People are still hurting along the Gulf Coast from Hurricane Katrina. Hundreds of thousands of lives have been changed forever. There are watches and warnings along the Atlantic Coast with concerns about Hurricane Ophelia. Because of the effects from Katrina, people are on edge. Our soldiers continue to fight in Iraq and Afghanistan. People are still dying from AIDS. People are still poor. People are still homeless.

September 13 is my birthday. My day started at 4:15 a.m. (My alarm was set for 4:45, but one of my Chihuahuas uses her twelve-year-old body as my alarm.) There will be good, bad, and some ugly thrown in throughout the day. My goal is to concentrate on the good. If it runs true to form, it will probably end around 6:30 in my recliner. No doubt about it, I live an exciting life.

On any given day, in any given month, in any given year, both good and bad things happen. Good seldom makes the news. Check it out. We cannot let evil dictate our actions and our attitudes. I remind us of the words of Jesus: "I have told you all this so that you may have peace in me. Here on earth you will have many trials and sorrows. But take heart, because I have overcome the world" (John 16:33 NLT).

Every day can be a good day. We can have peace because we know the Peacemaker. Enjoy your next birthday, no matter what aches and pains you may have or what problems you may face. God has overcome the world . . . and He's working on my knee.

lesson 40

For Some, Freedom Will Always Be a Verb

By any physical standards, he was an old man. The wrinkles, the stooped shoulders, the eyeglasses that were too big for his face, and the baseball cap that was too big for his head all gave him away. He stood silently with the help of a cane, high atop a bluff overlooking the ocean. His stare was focused on the horizon. It was as if he was searching for something specific, something tangible, but all he could see was a memory.

It was a struggle to control his emotions. He simply stood in silence, hearing only the crashing of the waves below and the echoes of his memories. The most difficult part of his journey was still to come. He turned and walked toward the cemetery. With each labored step, the emotions gathered momentum and the memories became more than echoes.

This time he was searching for something specific, a certain gravestone—but in this cemetery, all the gravestones looked alike.

40. For Some, Freedom Will Always Be a Verb

All had white crosses; only the names were different. He found the object of his search and slowly dropped to his knees. He ran his fingers over the name and cried. The last time he had seen his brother was on June 6, 1944, on the sand below, a horror known then as Omaha Beach.

"The long sobs of the violins of Autumn / Wounds my heart with a monotonous languor." This part of Paul Verlaine's nineteenth-century poem "Chanson d'automne," was the signal to the French Underground that the invasion of Europe was at hand, an event known as D-day, June 6, 1944. The scenario above has been played out for years as veterans have returned to French soil.

There is no question about French-American relations with the people of Normandy. American soldiers are still remembered as heroes and liberators. In one recent article, a seventy-seven-year-old resident of Normandy was quoted as saying, "We will never forget that the Americans gave us our freedom." Our soldiers understood freedom because they came from a free country and were determined to keep it that way. They did. Thousands lost their lives preserving it. Those are the ones we must remember.

D-day veterans come here to remember, and so do their children. By any physical standards, the man was in pretty good shape. Being a former Green Beret helped. The taut face, the straight back, the strong arms, the medals on his chest, and the beret fitting snugly on his head all gave him away. He stood on the bluff, overlooking Omaha Beach, his stare focused on the horizon. His thoughts were of photos and dreams of what might have been.

He turned and walked toward the cemetery. He found the object of his search, stopped, and stood silently. He had never met his father. This was the first time he had seen his grave. He ran his fingers over the name on the cross. It reminded him of the friends he had lost in the war in Vietnam. He stood erect. He saluted. He remembered. He cried.

For some, freedom will always be a verb. That's the sad part about freedom. It seems someone always has to die.

Chapter 5:
Give Me the Remote Control So I Can Change My Channel of Blessing

Lessons in Sharing the Gospel

You Don't Really Need Bait When You Fish for Carp

By nature, I am not a fisherman. The only thing I've fished for in recent years is compliments. I used to go fishing when I was younger and would sometimes catch a carp. They were not for eating . . . unless you lived in medieval times. Carp have a thick, mucous coating (like your cousin from northern Minnesota), and medieval cooks would boil it and mix it with spices to produce a gelatin that was used as a preservative. They also mixed carp eggs with almond milk curds to make cheese.

King Arthur eating carp eggs and milk curds would have created a different image of him sitting on his throne. In modern times, there is not much demand for carp. Some people in the world do eat them. Some people say they are good smoked. The problem is getting them to roll up with the paper. There is a correct process for eating them. Once the fish is cleaned, it must be descaled. If you are doing this alone, please use caution with D-flat major and B-minor.

Fish don't always act as they should. A man in Missouri was fishing out of his boat when a forty-pound carp flew out of the water and hit him in the chest. One woman in Illinois was riding her Jet Ski when a ten-pound carp jumped out of the water and knocked her over. A woman in Italy was riding her moped. She lost control when a giant carp jumped out of the canal next to the road and hit her in the face. All three victims tried to sue the local Game and Fish Commission. There was no history of aquatic law, so the cases were handled in small clams court.

I can't think of anything more humiliating than to be smacked in the face by a flying carp. Unless it would be the man in Ontario who was innocently doing some yard work when a two-pound bass fell out of the sky and hit him in the head. Authorities believe the fish was dropped by a wandering bird from the nearby lake. That's the ultimate in humiliation . . . struck by a bird dropping.

When I went fishing, I knew I was more powerful than the fish. I was not going to be intimidated by anything with scales, even my childhood piano teacher. I was determined to catch fish and have fun doing it. Likewise, we Christians have a mission. Go fish. Our bait may be a tract, or it may be our life's story. But we must go.

Fishing for carp is easy. Fishing for men is not. It takes effort and determination. Some of them are like carp—unloved and unwanted—and they may not always act as they should. They will not jump into the boat just because we are fishing. They may even humiliate us by smacking us in the face, literally or figuratively, when we confront them with the gospel.

We must go with the attitude that God is more powerful, and we are not going to be intimidated. It is our mission, and we must get involved . . . hook, line, and sinker.

I Understand the Cheese, but Tell Me That Empty Tomb Story

Contrary to what our instincts and preconceived notions may tell us, not all bizarre news stories have their origin in New York City. In Alaska, a seven-hundred-pound bull moose was found hanging by his antlers from a telephone line fifty feet in the air. Moose are migratory animals, and he was obviously upset at the portion of his long-distance phone bill that said "roaming charges."

A sixty-two-year-old man in a small town in Russia stopped an intruder in his home. He killed him by hitting him in the head with a large zucchini. In our house, the weapon of choice is usually Spam. In parts of China, one of the celebrations of the Chinese New Year includes watching a person feed a live snake into his mouth and out through his nose. I did that one time in college with meat loaf . . . unintentionally.

Religion is not exempt from sometimes carrying the "bizarre" tag. A cheese sandwich sold on eBay for $28,000. The owner, and apparently the buyer, thought they could see an image of Jesus in the cheese. Just doing his part of sharing the Gouda news. A pastor in Oklahoma once claimed to have seen a nine-hundred-foot Jesus standing next to his new church being constructed. He used the vision to raise millions of dollars for the project. If you are reading this and you are wealthy, I once saw an image of Jesus standing next to a Chevrolet Silverado 4x4 Crew Cab. I think it was red with a tan interior.

In New York City, a small religious group was in a spiritual uproar over what they considered to be a modern miracle. A fish cutter was about to club a twenty-pound carp at the local fish market when the carp started yelling at him in Hebrew. Being a typical male, the fish cutter panicked and ran screaming from the store. A woman would have realized instantly that a carp cannot speak Hebrew and that God would only have spoken through an angelfish.

Jesus lived what some would consider a bizarre life. He was born in a stable, His mother was a virgin, He touched lepers, He raised dead people back to life, He made blind eyes see (though He wasn't as successful with a few blind hearts), and He loved people. Oh yeah. There was one more thing: He walked on water.

One day, He was crucified on a cross. While He was on the cross, He forgave those who put Him there. Strange. Even the disciples didn't understand Him. After three days, it really got bizarre. He rose from the dead. Well, that's odd. No other prophet had done that. Then again, no other prophet had been God's Son.

That's the story of Easter. God sent His only Son to die for a lost world, including the people who rejected Him. It's only bizarre because it is a unique kind of love. Have you heard the one about Jesus and the empty tomb? Hmm. It seems strange that you aren't sharing it.

You Are Most Definitely a Winner (Until You Read the Fine Print)

This week my hair stands up with excitement, and my split ends join together in quiet celebration. Put on your Sunday best while I tell you . . . drum roll, please . . . that I was notified through the mail . . . please control your emotions . . . that I have been preapproved to be admitted into a correspondence school to become a pet groomer. At this point, there should be paws for reflection. I am stupefied. I am speechless. I didn't even know I had filled out an application form, and I certainly didn't know I could learn how to cut dog hair through the mail. I can't wait to try it out on one of my Chihuahuas.

My idea of pet grooming is to rinse off the dog in the sink, although I did try to brush her hair one time with Beverly holding her down. All she did was snarl . . . and the dog was none too pleased either. (A word of caution: there is no foolproof method for approaching a snarling Chihuahua. Come to think of it, there is no foolproof method for approaching a snarling wife either.) After her bath, I just raise up my Chihuahua in my hand like the Olympic torch and run around the yard until she dries. This was the main reason we had traded our Labrador retriever for a Chihuahua.

It is probably just a coincidence, but another exciting letter came in the same batch of mail. It seems a national magazine has carefully checked their records, through a special subatomic audit, and has confirmed that my family has never won a major prize in their sweepstakes. They are concerned. So am I. I could feel their pain as pity and concern began oozing out of their personal letter addressed to "Marlin K. Bladd." They even wanted to give me *two* chances to win! More oozing.

I was all set to order a really neat CD, *Snoop Dog Bug Zapper Rapper D Sings the Love Songs of Eddy Arnold,* when I got out my magnifying glass to read the little-bitty print at the bottom of the back page of the letter. My chances of winning were eighty duhzillion to one, and I had to buy 437 CDs over the next fifty-two years. Now I am beyond concerned. I am hurt. I am devastated. It is another bubble burst for the Bladd family.

I could not read these letters without thinking of some familiar words: "For God so loved the world that He gave His only begotten Son, that whoever believes in Him should not perish but have everlasting life" (John 3:16 NKJV). Talk about your ultimate preapproval! The notification was much more than a letter. It came in the form of a baby, sent special delivery to an unreceptive world.

In the sweepstakes of life, God freely sends His gift of love to everyone. We are to deliver the message. He preapproved His love for us just as we are, no strings attached. Hate the sin—love the sinner. Too many times in our efforts to explain God's offer, we try to make exceptions. There is only one problem with that approach. In God's offer, there is no fine print.

Come, Ye Sinners, Poor and Needy . . .
but Only on Sundays at Eleven

It was great being a child in the 1950s. It may have been peach-picking time in Georgia, but when I visited my grandmother in Arkansas it was always cheek-pinching time for her friends. It was also a time when I didn't have to see "reality" television shows, eat anything healthy, or be exposed to Super Bowl halftime shows. My biggest temptation was whether to shoot my dart gun at my grandmother's windows.

One of my fondest memories is reading the ads in the back of the comic books at the barbershop. One particular ad offered a set of Revolutionary War soldiers (two hundred pieces in all) for $1.99, and it was not available in any toy stores. I sent in my money with visions of a play set scattered all over the dining room. It arrived in six weeks . . . in a box about the size of an inexpensive hamster coffin. The soldiers were one inch tall. When set up, the whole thing covered an area the size of a large sucker. It was scattered all over a dinner plate. I was livid . . . and I didn't even know what the word meant.

As I got older, I looked up *livid* in the dictionary and tried not to be livid anymore. I get semi-livid today when I see similar ads ending with the phrase "not available in stores." Loosely translated, it means, "We tried selling this product in stores and no one would buy it—not even wrestling fans." One of them is for a wonder diet pill. It is so powerful you can lose an entire family in three months.

Another item not available in stores is Ladybug Land. It comes with a label that says, "Please allow two weeks for your larvae to develop." That's one phrase I can honestly say I've never used in a normal conversation. There is also a Butter Butler available. You mash a stick of butter into a tube and squeeze. It's supposed to eliminate the globs of butter or margarine that have built condos in your butter tray. It is also convenient, because if there is ever a murder in your house you can just say, "The butter did it."

What disturbs me most is manufacturers who come up with these great can't-live-without-it products and then limit the availability. Can you believe anyone would use that kind of marketing approach with an important product that should reach as many people as possible? Of course you can, because you and I are a part of the greatest marketing fiasco in Christendom—selling the kingdom of God to a lost world.

Some things never change. Grandmothers and their friends still pinch cheeks, and the church still tries to keep God inside a box. As the church, we offer the greatest life-changing event ever created; yet for years we have told an unsuspecting world that if they want to meet God, then come take a peek inside our box on Sunday mornings at eleven.

We need to let God out of the box and take Him to our friends, coworkers, and neighbors. As long as we continue to limit God's availability, fewer people will be answering our ads.

Hear the Music of the Beatles

Most of us hate pests. They bug us, they irritate us, they're creepy, and they're icky . . . and that only describes our younger brothers and sisters. Of course, I am kidding. We all love our siblings, and our children get along all the time. I am referring to literal insects that not only make us mad but also damage our property, which could also describe rude cousins.

One of these is the carpenter ant (not to be confused with the carpenter uncle), easily recognizable because of his many hit records. This is a large black ant that likes to chew wood products, very similar to a man who is tired of his wife's cooking. These ants leave little piles of sawdust wherever they bore a hole for entry. The easiest way to keep them from boring holes is to cut off the electricity so they cannot plug in their little drills. They like to nest in moist areas such as under the sink, in the laundry room, around my wife's mashed potatoes, or in my daughter's closet.

45. Hear the Music of the Beatles

Yesterday, when our troubles seemed so far away, there was an even more heinous invasion of unwanted pests. Some beetles made a return trip to the United States a couple of years ago. Unless you are a farmer, you probably didn't notice. These beetles played a different kind of music. They ate crops. These beetles did not have a ticket to ride, so they evidently became stowaways on a yellow submarine out of Japan.

They arrived in Middle Tennessee after taking a wrong turn on Abbey Road during a hard day's night. The beetles were told to get back, but eventually the bug police, led by Sergeant Pepper when he wasn't directing a lonely hearts club band, just decided to let it be.

The pests would come together and munch on apple trees, soybeans, Japanese maple trees, and even poison ivy, destroying each in the process. All the farmers could do was cry, "Help!" One farmer was asked how things were going in his battle against the pests. He realized they were going to be in his strawberry fields forever, and all he could say in frustration was, "I'm getting nowhere, man."

Unfortunately we hear that cry more and more every day, eight days a week. The people we meet may not verbalize it, but their actions speak volumes about where they are going spiritually. They are inundated by the pests of overwork, failure in relationships, financial problems, fear, and worry; and they are getting nowhere. They are not free as a bird. They are imprisoned by their circumstances. They are crying out. They are lonely and no one seems to care.

Do you want to know a secret? You don't have to be lonely, and Someone does care. You just sometimes need to slow down and listen to God. God loves you so much He sent His Son to die for you. All you need is love, the kind of love that only Jesus can give. As He did throughout His ministry, today, to people everywhere, He sends this message: "P.S. I love you."

Remember the Light, but Look Out for the Train

You may have missed this story. It was in the *Arkansas Democrat-Gazette* on November 10, 1994. Voters in Eureka Springs, Arkansas, elected a woman to the city council. She won by one vote. There was only one small problem. She was dead. She had died shortly before the election, but her name had to remain on the ballot.

The voters knew she was dead when they voted for her. Several voters told reporters that the televised debate did seem kind of one-sided. Some said she won the debate hands down. Others thought it was too close to call . . . a dead heat. The popular feeling was that a dead woman makes a better council member than a live man any day.

On the local scene, a newspaper reported that two dead cows on the side of a highway were ticketed by police officers. They had been dead so long their milk had turned to cottage cheese. They were charged with carrying a congealed weapon. You may have missed this story also. I cut it out of one of those tabloid newspapers several years ago. They cover nice human-interest stories like "700-Pound Nearsighted Man Marries an Elk," and "Farmer Plays National Anthem by Squeezing His Goose." They also seem to have more than their share of stories about people seeing images of dead loved ones in ordinarily inanimate objects like mashed potatoes. Other than a caulking gun, a lost sock, and one of our Chihuahuas, I have never seen anything in the mashed potatoes at our house.

I also read about this dog, Shep, that wandered into a small town in Montana with his owner back in 1936. When the owner died, his casket was placed on the eastbound train while Shep stood by whining and watching. The train left and Shep disappeared. However, every time a train pulled into the station, Shep would be there, wagging his tail and looking for his master's return.

There is another story you may have missed. It seems this person died between two other men on a hill outside the city of Jerusalem about two thousand years ago. He never won any elections, but He was a King. He was beaten for loving people and then crucified. He wasn't killed. He chose to die. There is a difference. After his death, He was placed in a tomb and everyone assumed that was where the story would end. Wrong assumption. Big mistake. It was only the beginning. His name was Jesus.

Ironic, isn't it? Some people today do not know He came the first time. Others stand around the train station debating when He will return. We Christians know what we should be doing to further His kingdom, but we spend too much time wagging our tongues and watching for the train . . . when we should be telling the story.

Doesn't It Hurt if You Have a Shoulder Drop-off?

The more I travel, the more convinced I am that people who write signs have a very precarious grip on the concept of reality. Then again, maybe the grip I thought I had is finally slipping. I saw one highway sign that said, "Slow Dip." If describing someone's personality, that could be an oxymoron. It could also describe an appetizer at an imbecile party. I know some drivers are none too smart, but do we need a road sign to tell us that? Another sign that has always bothered me is "Loose Gravel." Isn't all gravel, by definition, loose? I have never seen tight gravel.

Here's another one that bugs me: "Shoulder Drop-off." If we drop them off by nine, can we pick them up at three? What about the sign that says, "Bridge May Ice in Cold Weather"? Do they really think it may ice in *warm* weather? Another one said, "Moose Load." I never saw the moose load, and I'm thankful.

Then there are those signs that make you stop and have a pondering moment. On one trip, I saw one that said, "Caution: Hidden Driveway." Why would someone hide their driveway? Are they afraid it might get stolen, or is it just an embarrassment to the neighborhood?

One place had a sign out front that said, "Shrimp in Store." Sure enough, the guy behind the counter was only three feet tall. I saw a water tower advertising a local restaurant, the Blue Hereford. Except for a bizarre college cafeteria experiment involving less-than-adequate preservatives, I have never personally seen a blue cow—although I once passed a cattle truck bound for the slaughterhouse and heard some cows singing the blues.

I went through a town by the name of Imboden. Isn't that what buildings do when you blow them up from the inside? As in the news story headline, "Trucker Eats Five-Pound Crab-and-Cucumber Casserole; Three People Dead from Resulting Imboden." My favorite was the "State Trout-Rearing Unit." What do we do with the out-of-state trout, and what exactly is involved in rearing a trout?

Signs can also be misleading. On another trip, I crossed the White River. It was blue. I crossed the Black River. It was brown. I crossed the Red River. It was green. It was all rather confusing. It reminded me of Christians who have bumper stickers that say, "Jesus is Lord." Then they drive like a maniac to beat you to a parking spot at the mall. Jesus seems to be Lord over everything except driving etiquette.

We Christians are sometimes rather confusing creatures. We wear the usual signs such as crosses, WWJD bracelets, and going to church on Sunday, but it doesn't seem to change the way we live during the week. We don't need to send confusing signals. The way some of us act, if our churches were a commercial for Christianity I'm not convinced anyone would ever buy our product. If that ever happens, we might as well put a sign on the church that says, "Going out of Business."

What Happens When You Squeeze a Chihuahua?

I have taken CPR (Comical Pastoral Resuscitation) classes on two occasions. After each one, I was certified to save people for twelve months . . . especially if they looked like a department-store mannequin and had a plastic hose sticking out of their chest, clear plastic wrap over their mouth, and a permanent smile. In layman's terms, it simply meant I was qualified to jump on top of people, pinch their nostrils, blow into their mouth, and beat their chest.

It is similar to what they do at weddings in some isolated areas of West Texas instead of exchanging vows. This kind of training comes in handy when you happen upon someone who is choking (like the '86 Red Sox) or someone suffering from cardiac arrest, where the heart is stopped for making a U-turn. It is not to be confused with Gomer's condition on the *Andy Griffith Show*, which was called "citizen's arrest."

What's really scary about this whole CPR thing is that it can be used on pets. Now don't get me wrong; I love my dogs. But the mental picture of me putting my mouth on one of them is wrong on so many levels. One of my Chihuahuas, Molly, is eleven years old. Her breath always smells like she just ate a walrus. I don't want to put my finger in her mouth to clear out any foreign objects. She's not from around here. Of course there are foreign objects. And I don't want to pinch her nostrils and blow into her mouth. She'd bite me.

Tiny, our secondary Chihuahua, is even smaller. If I blew into her mouth, she'd blow up. And what's this business about giving them the Heimlich maneuver if they are choking? There's another picture I don't want the neighbors to see: me squeezing a Chihuahua. If I squeezed Tiny like that without a firm hold, she'd shoot across the room.

We probably don't have many occasions to give CPR to people in trouble, but we more than likely see people every day who need a jump-start on their spiritual hearts. We may see them simply by looking in the mirror. It is amazing what a breath of fresh air can do for the stale and stagnant heart in getting rid of obstructions. Know anyone who is choking on the food offered by the world when all they need is to taste the Bread of Life?

What they need is CPR—Christ-Promised Refuge. Jesus said, "Come to me, all you who are weary and burdened, and I will give you rest" (Matthew 11:28). "Let anyone who is thirsty come to me" (John 7:37 NRSV). "I have come that they may have life, and have it to the full" (John 10:10).

All are promising words from Jesus about rest, refuge, and resuscitation. We need to share them with others. When we do share, we can't ignore the "Chihuahuas" in life, those who may appear to be the most disgusting. We can't be choosy.

Are you trained in CPR? If you are a Christian, you are . . . and the world is your classroom.

I Never Saw the Bill,
but God Left the Light On in Damascus

Before seeing the light and becoming a minister of education, I spent twenty-four years in youth ministry. During those somewhat muddled years, I discovered two fascinating facts about teenagers. Number one, they are moody, which prepares them for marriage. Number two, they are aliens from another planet, which prepares them for in-laws. What else would explain their music, language, and hairstyles?

I do not wish to alarm any unsuspecting parents (Is that term an oxymoron?), but as soon as your child turns thirteen, he is taken by aliens and replaced by a mutation. He only appears to be human, much like the cast of *Saved by the Bell*. We notice the changes during this time, but we just blame it on the teenage years or whichever political party is in office.

Little do we know that the person sleeping in the pigpen down the hall has green blood, webbed feet, a light in his index finger, and a really good reason for never phoning home. Most of them return to human form at the age of eighteen, but a few mutations do slip into adulthood, which would explain the latest *Austin Powers* movie, people who eat sushi, and the man who invented diet food bars.

The other interesting thing I discovered about teenagers is their extreme susceptibility to popular trends and trendy evangelists. Their eating habits follow that pattern. A recent survey of teenagers indicated 25 percent of them said being a vegetarian would be cool. Of course this is the same survey that showed 50 percent of the teenagers thought a vegetarian was a doctor who worked on animals.

A couple of the evangelists I exposed my youth to had rather colorful testimonies about what their life was like before they met Christ, things even worse than what we see on those television reality shows. God obviously worked a miracle in their lives, but their stories were almost too colorful and exciting. Sometimes those testimonies left my youth questioning their salvation because their own testimonies were not quite as exotic.

One of the great stories in the New Testament is the conversion of Paul after he was blinded by a light on the road to Damascus. My experience was similar. I became a Christian in a small church in Little Rock, Arkansas, that had light and was located a few blocks from a road that led to the town of Damascus. The main differences are that the light was provided by a series of seventy-five-watt bulbs and I was nine years old.

While we are not all converted by a "Damascus Road" experience, we are all changed by the same Light. For some it is blinding, but for others it is more of a reflection of the Son, learning about Jesus while growing up in church. We all have a song, written by the same Master Composer. The verses may be different, but the chorus is always the same . . . "Jesus saves!"

Wait a Minute, Nobody Said Anything about Two Lawyers

Spring is here, and that can only mean one thing . . . college football has begun spring practice. That can only mean one thing . . . college football coaches around the country are speaking in footballese, and all we can do is scratch our collective heads. And some of our heads do need collecting. One coach said, "You can't take for granted the little things like getting in and out of the huddle." Maybe the scout team could help them find the huddle.

Another somewhat dubious quote was, "The guys really got out here and got after it for just having helmets on." I'm not sure I want to see that. Another coach said, "Pretty much everybody took a step forward." If they repeated that over and over, wouldn't they be doing the Hokey Pokey? My favorite quote was, "We are mainly concerned about personnel, putting people in the right position and executing what we do put in." I don't know that much about football, but won't it severely reduce the number of players available if they start executing them?

We can laugh at what coaches have actually said, but we can also laugh at what famous people probably said when there was no reporter around to record it. Alexander Graham Bell's first words on the telephone were actually, "If you would like to speak to Mr. Bell, please press one." George Orwell said to his psychiatrist, "I don't know, Doc. It's my older brother. He's always watching me." Noah must have said, "Wait a minute. Nobody said anything about two lawyers."

Johann Sebastian Bach's mother once said to him on the family farm, "Johann, before you go to bed, make sure all the horses are in the chorale." John Merrick, better known as the Elephant Man, actually said, "I am not an animal! I've just been on this committee too long!" Very few people realize that Victor Hugo's most popular literary character of all time, Quasimodo, was credited with this long-forgotten but remarkably insightful quote: "If I can just get past Wednesday, I think I'll be over the hump."

Have you ever thought about how things might be different if Jesus had responded to situations with another choice of words? During the storm on the Sea of Galilee, Jesus could have just said, "Man the lifeboats!" When the five thousand needed feeding, He could have said, "They should have thought of that before they came here."

How good are we at choosing our words wisely? Do we tell little lies to get us out of certain situations? If someone needs encouragement, do we offer it or do we remain silent? When troubles come our way, do we ask God to give us peace or do we scream for the lifeboats? If a friend comes to us in trouble, do we comfort him or just tell him he should have thought about the consequences before he made his choice?

I hope I never hear Jesus say, "I am the light of the world . . . but no one seems to be reflecting it."

Chapter 6:
If You Are Early to Bed and Early to Rise, You'll Probably Miss Your Teenager Coming Home

Lessons on Family Living

After the Music Ends, a Mother's Song Can Still Be Heard

I will give you a few clues, and you name the holiday started by Anna Jarvis in 1908. She came up with the idea to honor her mother, who helped wounded men on both sides of the Civil War, maintained a household, was a peacemaker, and took a covered wagon full of kids to soccer practice at 3:00 and then piano at 6:00. She never complained to her husband about him always sitting in the recliner with a remote control, a bag of chips, and a lazy Chihuahua.

Did you guess April Fools' Day? You were close, and you should be ashamed for thinking it. The correct answer is Mother's Day. Anna came up with the idea in church, where a lot of great ideas usually die, but this one survived. President Woodrow Wilson, who owned a chain of floral shops and a catfish house, made it official. It is the biggest dining-out day of the year and the day with the most long-distance collect calls.

51. After the Music Ends, a Mother's Song Can Still Be Heard

Oddly enough, it was intended as a day of honor, not a day of profit. Anna Jarvis wanted to honor the memory of her mother. Mothers need to be honored. My parents always took their vacation in the summer so my mother could visit her mother in Colorado, one time a year. My mother always cried when we left Colorado. I didn't understand why. I thought it was the mountains. Colorado is still my favorite place in the world.

When I was a baby, my mother rocked me and sang to me. It was soothing. As a young child, I got scared during severe thunderstorms. It wasn't long before I climbed into bed with my mom. Dad was OK, but he snored. This time my mother didn't sing, but I felt her music. I wasn't scared anymore.

As an older child playing baseball, I didn't always pitch perfect games. During one particularly bad outing, the other team began making fun of me. I shed a few tears and looked into the stands. My mother was smiling and clapping, but I also noticed tears on her face. I felt her arms around me, and I could hear her song. I felt good, but I didn't understand her tears.

I went off to college and my mother cried. I didn't understand why. I thought she was silly. When I got lonely I called home, collect. I got that hug over the phone, some encouragement, and felt her music. Several years later I married Beverly, and my mother cried at the wedding. (Not because of Beverly.) Again with the silliness. I assumed she wasn't pleased with the soloists.

My mother has been gone five years. I understand things now. A child may be the one injured, whether physically or psychologically, but a mother always feels the pain and shares the scar. I miss the hugs, the smiles, and even the tears, but I can still hear her song of love.

All through my ministry, I have felt the hugs and sensed the smiles. Whenever I love my family, I hear my mother's music. The old saying is accurate . . . a mother's work never really ends. Thank God, neither does her song.

Everyone Wins When Cheer Goes against the Tide

In what has to be the understatement of the year, in her early teens my daughter, Meredith, was a cheerleader. You have not really lived until you have survived in a house with a fourteen-year-old cheerleader. I could communicate extremely well with Meredith . . . if I had her permission.

Communication always worked best when I remembered the number one communication rule in parenting: the parent does all of the listening and must realize that anything the parent says will absolutely be the all-time dumbest words that any parent has ever uttered since the dawn of man, or at least since Cain and Abel complained about what their parents were wearing.

The biggest obstruction to healthy communication occurred when she transmutated into her Stepford Wives–like cheerleader mode. I found myself transported into a seldom-survived dimension of quasi-communication and supersized hyperactivity that moved at warp speed beyond the comprehension capabilities of average parents. I had inescapably entered the Cheerleader Zone.

The Cheerleader Zone is not for the squeamish parent. There are days when you just want to squeam. Even normal household activities such as looking in the mirror, carrying on a conversation, and walking through the house become grandiose productions because each event is injected with clenched fists, flailing arms, kicking legs, and a bobbing ponytail. When she had cheerleader friends over, it was like a bobblehead convention, and the dogs were none too pleased with eight screaming, bobbing fourteen-year-old girls cheering them on while trying to do their doggy business.

I attended her games and watched her lips move during a cheer. The words that came out did not match the formation of her mouth, and it was like watching a foreign movie with misspelled English subtitles. It was all cute and innocent until I watched her being violently flipped fifty feet in the air with no safety net and only two other fourteen-year-old girls to catch her. The parent in me wanted to scream; the male in me wanted to take charge and insist Beverly go out there and do something about it. Fortunately the patient, calm minister in me prevailed and reminded me I was sitting next to one of my best friends . . . who was also a really good doctor.

If the cheerleaders have done their job, everyone feels great when they finish their performance. You see, cheerleaders are encouragers. They play a vital role during the game. Oh, they never actually play the game, but they encourage those who do and those who watch. It's kind of like that in church. Most church members choose simply to watch the game, some will play, and some will cheer and encourage.

52. Everyone Wins When Cheer Goes against the Tide

Cheer cleanses our soul and makes us feel good. Cheer encourages while criticism depresses. Proverbs 15:13 says, "A happy heart makes the face cheerful, but heartache crushes the spirit." We all like to be encouraged, but it sometimes seems criticism comes easier and is more popular.

Cheer always freshens and brightens someone's day. Have you cheered for anyone lately? Cheer may go against the tide, but it's always great detergent for the soul . . . yours and theirs.

Pausing for a Few Senior Moments on the Road of Life

I t's that time of year again. Like Baptist preachers at a 1970s leisure-suit sale, pomp and circumstance is popping up everywhere. This inundation of pomp and circumstance has caused me to rent a bulldozer and get the dust off my old high-school yearbook from 1970, my senior year. I looked in the back of the book under "Senior Activities." Next to my name was "Beta Club, Key Club, All-District Band, Spanish Club, and Most Likely to Lose His Hair."

I remember being in the band and tooting my own horn, but I don't remember much about the others. The only thing I remember about Spanish Club is getting caught dancing one day before our meeting. I grabbed a handful of artificial grapes off of the teacher's desk and stuck them to my face. Then I stuck a banana in my mouth, grabbed a pair of maracas, and performed the

Mexican Hat Dance for the class. When the teacher arrived, she was not impressed. She thought her fruit salad had exploded. I realized then that my future was not in the performing arts, especially if I had to perform with artificial fruit.

I'm sure that in 1970 my parents were wondering where the years had gone. Parents today are wondering the same thing. Children in our church, barely potty-trained, are graduating from high school this month. Where did the years go? Wasn't it just last summer I took some of this year's seniors to children's camp? I even became like a mother to one of them, a boy named John who threw up on me. Time really does fly, and there are times when I wish its plane would be delayed. This is one of those times.

Every parent knows it is coming, but it doesn't make it any easier. We knew they were graduating from preschool. We still cried. We knew when they were going to walk from the car to their first day of kindergarten. We still cried. We knew one year later they would go to first grade. We cried. Then came middle school. We cried. Then it was learning to drive. Some of us cried more than others.

We dread or look forward to this day for eighteen years. We still cry. God seems to have a way of using tears to help wash away the pain of watching our children grow up. As the pain of graduation subsides, He moves the memories of yesterday to one side of our hearts and makes room for the dreams of tomorrow. We go through the cycle again, for as long as we have children we will have tears.

High-school graduation, like kindergarten, first grade, and middle school, is another speed bump on the road of life for parents. It causes us to slow down and reflect on the many blessings God has given us. Congratulations, seniors. You have been a blessing. Personally, I will miss you. You have made me miss youth ministry, but at the same time you made me thankful I am no longer in it. I am too old for the tears.

I will miss you, but I will have good memories. Twenty-five years from now, you probably won't remember much about high school. That's OK. It really doesn't matter where you've been or where you go . . . as much as where you stand.

The Best Stage for a Teenager Is the One That's Leaving Town

Most of us have been teenagers at one time or another. I have seen a few eleven- and twelve-year-olds who did not see the need of going through adolescence and morphed immediately into adulthood, much to the chagrin of their parents; but the rest of us faced teenage years. They are difficult years, made more difficult by the increasing number of fast-food restaurants available for them to choose from.

For those parents fortunate enough to have a living organism in their home with a seventeen-year-old body, a thirteen-year-old brain, and pants that hang down below their Twilight Zone, I have listed the various stages of growth. I hope this helps you to better understand your teenager, or at least helps you decide what size pants to buy.

Harry Potter Stage: At this stage in your teen's life, he still respects you and listens to what you say and is never moody. He can't wait to go to youth Bible study. He has the utmost concern for family, especially siblings, and loves to visit the grandparents. He loves for you to hug him publicly and is never embarrassed by the noises Grandpa sometimes accidentally makes while walking in the mall. Parents, read my lips. This is fiction! This stage does not exist!

Beaver Cleaver/Opie Taylor Stage: During this period, your teenager can do no wrong. If he does do wrong, he is so cute you don't want to punish him. You are just thrilled you don't have to go to Chuck E. Cheese's anymore. He still thinks like a child and believes you when you give him a curfew. He really does listen to you and doesn't think you came from Mars. Enjoy this stage. It usually only lasts about a week.

Industrial-Strength Acne Medicine Stage: What you see on the outside is just a cover-up for the turmoil happening inside. It's like a bad taco. You're never really sure of what's inside. Your teen is changing fast, physically and emotionally. To say he has a slight temper is to say that Vesuvius has a tendency to boil. It is as if a colony of crazed hormones hijacked two roller coasters, filled them with caffeine, and are playing demolition derby inside his body . . . without air bags. The only way for the teen to survive this stage is for the parents to be there when the roller coaster crashes.

The 699 Club Stage: During this stage your teenager wants to be a committed Christian but can't quite get over the hump. He's still a teen, but he wants to be an adult. He can't quite make the connection between rights and responsibilities. He wants to study his Bible, but there are other things that get in his way. Talking negatively about people at church is something he knows he is not supposed to do, but there are times when he just can't help it. He knows about giving to God, but he can't put it into practice. Sometimes church is only important to him when it is convenient.

Funny, isn't it? This stage is also referred to as adulthood.

Going Back to Malvern

D o you have a place you like to visit now and then that has pleasant memories of your childhood? Maybe it's the town where you grew up or maybe the town where your grandparents lived. For me, it is Malvern, Arkansas. My paternal grandparents lived there. Technically they were my grandmother and stepgrandfather, but who gets technical when you're a child?

Their names were Jessie and Jack. To me they were Grandma and Jack. I never got around to calling him Grandpa. We had an agreement. He called me Martin Keith, and I called him Jack. It worked pretty well. I spent a week or two with them every summer after my baseball season was over in Little Rock, about forty miles away.

Malvern was just like any small town in the 1950s. It was part Norman Rockwell and part Norman Bates. As a kid, I never noticed the struggle between the two identities. My world consisted of the area between my grandparents' home on Baker Street and downtown. Life was pretty simple.

Jack left early in the morning to go to work in the mine outside of Magnet Cove. He returned home around 3:30 and we had supper promptly at 4:00, always containing something fried and something sweet. In those days, people actually washed dishes and then it was time for a few rounds of dominoes (the game, not the pizza), a television show or two, and then closing the night with an hour on the front porch.

I loved sitting on the porch. I usually had my dart gun (rubber-tipped darts that would stick to metal) and would shoot at some toy soldiers set up on the porch. Sometimes I even shot at the metal swing because it made a perfect target. So did my grandparents. They moved to the other side of the porch. We just talked and had fun, and I sneaked a couple of shots at their legs. I could get away with a lot more at their house than I could at home.

One of my favorite things to do was taking the one-mile walk with my grandmother from the house to downtown. That was before Wal-Mart and before the interstate, so everything was downtown. My favorite store was Ben Franklin's Five & Dime (a variety store and toy central). It had a selection of darts and toy soldiers you wouldn't believe. It was almost as much fun as riding with Jack in his 1952 Chevy to take the trash to the dump. Coming back, he'd cut the engine halfway down the street and we would coast the rest of the way to the house.

I went through Malvern a few months ago on my way to Tennessee from New Mexico. Jack and Jessie are long gone. The house is in disrepair, the garage is in bad shape, and the hedge along the sidewalk is gone. But the porch is still there.

I had fun with my grandparents. They reinforced values I

learned at home like being nice to people, loving my country, loving God, and showing kindness when anger would be easier . . . simple, but profound. Do you have a Malvern? Life can still be simple. Be nice. Be kind. Love God. Love your country.

What about you? Do you shoot darts without rubber tips at others? Are you coasting through life with no power? Are you so busy you have forgotten some of your priorities? Return to Malvern. Well, you really can't go back to Malvern, but thank God, Malvern will always come back to you.

Tractor Pulls, Worship, and Other Dead Weight

To say I was present in the delivery room when my children were born has all the impact of saying there were shower stalls on the *Titanic*. In the end, neither of us was actually needed. With Meredith, Beverly had the audacity to go into labor during an important Southwest Conference basketball game, on the television in the labor room, between Arkansas and Texas A&M. She and her pit crew did fine with me just standing there with my best Gomer Pyle–like expression that said, "Gawll-eee, I don't think I've ever seen anything like that before!"

I was the epitome of dead weight. I felt Beverly's pain as she squeezed my wrist. I almost dropped the remote control. It was probably best I was not needed because I had several important chromosomes—the ones containing patience, understanding, and a strong stomach—that had been placed on the inactive list when she went into labor. They returned when we got Meredith home from the hospital but then mysteriously disappeared when she became a teenager.

Three years later, things were going to be different with David. I was a veteran, and Beverly's timing was much better because it was October and a Thursday. At that time, football was only on Saturday, Sunday, and Monday. Everything went fine. But since he was a boy, I knew one day I would have to have that special talk about a certain subject every father has to discuss with his son. I dreaded it. He had seen it on television and kept asking questions. What could I do? I had to take him to his first truck and tractor pull.

This is a contest where horribly disfigured decal-infested vehicles compete by pulling a load of dead weight across the dirt. This is not to be confused with a funeral procession in some parts of Missouri. It was a very entertaining evening, if you could get past the nausea-inducing odor . . . and that was just from the people sitting around us. The odor from the tractors was worse.

In an odd sort of way, it reminded me of church—not the odor of those around us but how we prepare ourselves for the worship experience. Is it something that we really look forward to, or do we dread it and only go to please someone else? Do we go planning to participate, or do we expect to be entertained?

Do we inadvertently reach for a remote control to change part of the service we don't like? Do we spend more time looking around than we do looking inward? True worship is birthed through the heart. Do we ever go into a worship service with an expectant heart?

There are two ways we can approach worship. We can go with the psalmist, who said, "I was glad when they said to me, 'Let us go to the house of the LORD'" (Psalm 122:1 NASB). Our other choice is to enter with the pessimist, who says, "Come on, honey, we gotta go to church. Let's go see what we can find wrong today." If we choose the second approach, maybe we would be better off at a tractor pull . . . with the rest of the dead weight.

When God Goes to Kansas, You'd Better Be in His Rearview Mirror

I remember vacations to Colorado taken in a 1957 Dodge sedan, and later a 1964 Rambler station wagon. These were the years between ox-drawn wagons and minivans. For that preinterstate ordeal I was armed only with seven hundred comic books, a couple of travel games purchased by hopeful parents, some sour candy, a hundred toy cars and trucks, and a brother.

One of the neat things about traveling to Colorado was going through Kansas (state motto: "Will work for trees"). Like its sister states Nebraska, Arkansas, and Delaware, Kansas doesn't get the respect it deserves. The first four letters of those states spells "dank," as in describing someone's basement. (It could also stand for "don't actually need Kentucky.")

If you look at a map of the United States, were it not for Kansas, Missouri and Colorado would be short and squatty. *The Wizard of*

Oz was set in Kansas. Thank goodness. If Dorothy had said, "Toto, I don't think we're in New Jersey anymore," who would have cared? (Odd historical note: When filming began, there were no witches in Kansas. They had to be imported from Massachusetts.)

When our giddy forefathers drew the borders for the states, apparently with an Etch-a-Sketch after a few mugs of rum, Kansas was placed in the unenviable position of being next door to Colorado. For years, people have simply tolerated Kansas while on their way to Colorado. This is unacceptable. It's like playing with your salad before eating your steak or tolerating the black part of the Oreo cookie to get to the icing.

Kansas can stand on its own. The world's deepest hand-dug well is in Greensburg, right next door to the world's largest pile of dirt. Hugoton is the home of the largest natural gas field in the world. Not coincidentally, it is adjacent to the largest stockyard in the United States. Of course, the most famous person from Kansas is Matt Dillon. Marshal Dillon roamed the streets of Dodge City for more than twenty years. He was most noted for drinking beer with Doc and Festus and not kissing Miss Kitty.

I have fond memories of traveling through Kansas on our way to Colorado. It was fun. I had things to keep me busy, and I enjoyed the tourist stuff. It was all part of vacation. I didn't wait until I got to Colorado to have fun. Too bad adults don't think like children. We sometimes want to put off serving God until we get from this point to the next point. We will begin tithing when we get a better job or a promotion. We will serve next year. We'll do our part down the road.

Sometimes that road goes on forever. We put God off long enough, and we end up not serving at all. The road really does become less traveled because we never get on it. Too many of us have disregarded our spiritual road map and are simply waiting to serve God until we reach Colorado, when all the while God needs us in Kansas.

Wherever your "Kansas" is, God is there, looking at His road map . . . and wondering where you are.

HOME

Homecoming Is Where the Heart Was

I went to homecoming at Ouachita Baptist University in November 1995. It was my twenty-year reunion. The first observation I made was that all college students look fifteen years old. The second observation I made was how much everyone else in my class had changed in twenty years. Other than gaining forty pounds and losing most of my beautiful hair, I had changed very little. When some people saw me for the first time in twenty years, they got that "Is that your body, or did the Pillsbury Doughboy explode?" look on their faces.

That brings me to what I call "Martin's First Law of Homecomings." It states that the amount of fun you have at a college homecoming is directly proportional to the amount of time that elapses between the moment a friend who has not seen you in twenty years spots you and the first derogatory remark that comes out of his mouth about your waistline, hairline, or facial lines . . . or something along those lines.

The football stadium at Ouachita is constructed in such a manner that to get to your seat, you must walk down what seems like a three-mile-long sidewalk in front of the entire home side of the field. The first two or three homecomings I attended after graduation were real ego-feeders because enough students there recognized me and would yell out my name in front of fifty thousand screaming college kids and sleepy alumni. (It was probably a shorter walk and closer to two thousand people, but when you are twenty-three, a recent college graduate, and home from Texas, everything seems bigger.)

That brings me to "Martin's Second Law of Homecomings." It says that the number of people screaming out your name (or even physically able to do so) as you walk in front of the stands in full view of everyone decreases as the number of years since your graduation increases. Twenty years had gone by, and no one was screaming my name.

I have discovered over the years, like the apostle Paul, to be content in whatever state I find myself . . . although New Jersey would be pushing it. My college years were great, and I would not trade them for anything; but neither do I want to go back. The past is a wonderful place to visit, and I do very often, but I do not want to live there. No, nobody called my name in front of all the fans to feed my ego that year. But that's OK. For you see, homecoming is where my heart *was*—but in twenty years, my heart had moved.

My head could not have been bigger, because walking at my side in front of all those people was my almost thirteen-year-old daughter, of whom I was very proud. No one screamed out my name in front of all those people, but Meredith, walking by my side, did say, "I love you, Daddy."

When I returned home, my eleven-year-old son, David, greeted me with, "Hi, Dad!" (extremely wordy for him) and a hug. Then it was my thirty-something wife with "Hi, Dad!" (extremely normal for her) and another hug. And through those three moments in time—a long walk and two hugs—my homecoming was made complete.

Nothing Changes Your Outlook Like a Perspective from the Pimple

How long has it been since you had a good case of the goose bumps? I am not referring to the kind you get watching a horror movie, or when you walk into the local revenue office to renew your car tags, or when someone comes to your house at Halloween disguised as your high-school principal. Those are all fear-related.

I am talking about the kind of goose bumps you get when you see or hear something that reminds you of an experience from the past, and it overwhelms you with emotion. It's like the reaction I get when I look at my wedding pictures and see my hair. I get this powerful urge to comb something.

I have had severe cases of goose bumps while walking through the Alamo in San Antonio, Texas. I thought about all those men and women who survived for thirteen days and gave their lives for

Texas's independence. I had goose bumps while standing on the USS *Arizona* memorial in Pearl Harbor. I thought about the men who died on that ship on December 7, 1941. I've read the names on the Vietnam Veterans Memorial in Washington. It gave me chills.

Most of my goose bumps, though, pop up whenever I think about my childhood and teenage years and spending a two-week vacation with my parents in Colorado. This was our only opportunity to visit my nocturnal grandparents (those are grandparents on the mother's side who don't go out after dark). My grandparents lived in Florence, Colorado, a small town about thirty miles southwest of Colorado Springs. We followed the same path that the pioneers used 150 years ago in their passage west looking for religious freedom, the newest Wal-Mart opening, and a territory free of professional wrestling. Along this same path, they also found a territory free of trees.

My parents did not have a lot of money, but they made sure my brother and I had many fun experiences, whether it was a vacation, a picnic, a walk in the park, or a baseball game. Sometimes it was just going with my dad on a business trip. They weren't expensive or extravagant trips, but you can't buy those kinds of memories with money.

What kind of memories are you building with your kids? Have you made a commitment to spend some time with your family? It's never too late. Doctors tell us that acne in teenagers can be irritated by stress. When was the last time your teenager was awed by anything other than television, DVDs, Mp3s, CDs, video games, or music videos? Has your child's sense of wonder been replaced by your teenager's wonder of cents?

Are we providing opportunities for our kids to relieve the stress, or are we causing it? If I'm going to cause bumps on my children, I hope it is the goose kind, not the pimple kind. How long has it been since your teenager had a case of the goose bumps? Here is a question each of us needs to ask ourselves as families in the new millennium: are we geared for goose bumps, or are we programmed for pimples?

Riding in Style on a Trip Down Memory Lane

On October 11, 1975, *Saturday Night Live* debuted with George Carlin as guest host. In those early years it was a classic. On October 11, 1984, Kathryn Sullivan became the first woman to perform a space walk. She was an astronaut aboard the space shuttle *Challenger.* On October 11, 1984, David Babb was born at Baptist Hospital in Little Rock, Arkansas. He is our son. In those early years he was a classic, launching baby food into orbit and presenting a real challenge at mealtime. His mother went into orbit.

David's favorite toys growing up were Micro Machines and LEGOs. He spent hours playing with them in his room. I spent hours shopping for the newest version at the Toys "R" Bigger Than Us store. At least I didn't feel out of place like I did when searching for Meredith's Cabbage Patch dolls or My Little Ponies. When it came time to play with the LEGOs, David never bothered with instructions. While I was busy trying to find the English version, he was halfway through the castle, boat, fire station, or whichever current space weapon he could use to shoot his sister with the death ray.

As a child, David pretty much kept to himself. He really didn't begin talking to us until he reached the tenth grade. Before that time he communicated through a series of hoots, snarls, twitches, and grunts. We just told friends and grandparents he watched a lot of Tarzan movies.

His favorite sport was baseball. He was a left-handed pitcher who threw strikes. For practice I nailed a white paper plate to the house in the backyard, about the height of an eight-year-old's strike zone. He was a fanatic. We went through a ton of white paper plates. We went to a church potluck, and he wiped out a whole row of senior adults when they held up their plates. He was good. Of course we had to tape a white paper plate to the catcher's mitt during games, but that made it a genuine home plate.

He was so efficient in one game the opposing coach accused him of using performance-enhancing drugs. Can you believe that? Our lawyer, with the firm of Hoots, Snarls, Twitches, and Grunts, advised us to agree to the test. We did. He tested positive for gummy worms.

Recently we celebrated his twenty-first birthday. He is in college at East Tennessee State University. Is this really his third year? He still doesn't read instructions, but he seems to have followed those of his parents pretty well. The toy cars have been replaced by a Mustang, and the building blocks are now musical instruments.

Where has the time gone? It seems like only yesterday he was fighting with his sister. Come to think of it, that *was* yesterday . . . except he no longer shoots her with the death ray. They actually talk to each other. Once in a while, I venture into his closet. Just beyond the old baseball glove and hat, there is a box in the corner. It is full of old toys. I take a few of them out and think about old times. I reminisce. I smile. I cry. I ponder for a while. I move on.

If you are a parent, you know the drill. I guess you could call it taking a trip down memory lane, but I call it driving Micro Machines through LEGOland. It was a wonderful ride.

Chapter 7:
Everything You Always Wanted to Know about Heroes, but Couldn't Find on Reality Television

Lessons from Real People

Some Things Really Are Done Too Soon

My first foray into fatherhood began in January 1982. I remember it like it was yesterday, but I'm a little fuzzy on when I got up from the floor. I do remember watching the basketball game in the delivery room as I encouraged Beverly during the labor. My first thought was, *Hey, watching basketball on a large-screen TV and holding Beverly's hand while she does all the work . . . This fatherhood stuff is OK!* Then we got Meredith home from the hospital, and everything changed. I kept wondering where the instructions were for this thing.

The sequel to our first child arrived in October 1984. There was nothing pressing on television, so I was ready and willing to hold hands again. There was a lot of screaming and yelling, but after I calmed down, everything went fine. Beverly went natural, and I had an epidural. When we got David home from the hospital, I was an old pro at changing diapers, so I thought I was ready. But I was not ready for boys. Boys can aim. Every day was a monsoon season. It was another one of those moments when instructions would have been appreciated.

With our firstborn, we had seventeen volumes of pictures and kept a microscope on her physical health. With David, we used one disposable camera and pretty much let him roam freely with Taco, our Chihuahua.

We were told about the joy and happiness children bring but were never warned about the tears—theirs and ours. Parents seem to go through long cycles of happiness and tears. Sometimes one leads to the other. With Meredith, there was the first day of school, the first dance recital, trying out for cheerleader, learning to drive, and graduation. With David, there was the first day of school, the first game as a pitcher in baseball, moving to a new school in another state, finally learning to talk in the tenth grade, and graduation. Has it really been that many years? They grew up too fast. I wonder sometimes if children grow up at the speed of parenting.

I think I hear my father in the background saying, "I told you so." Kids may grow up too fast, but sometimes parents go away too soon. I buried my father on June 18, 1994, the day before Father's Day, on what would have been his eighty-first birthday. He did live eighty years, but for me it was still too soon. My parents raised me in church. My father taught me to have a sense of humor and to live life to the fullest, no matter what the circumstances may be. It's biblical.

When I was a child, we used to go on picnics. On one particular day the flies were terrible, and I was swatting away. My father finally looked over at me and said, "Martin Keith, if you spend all your time swattin' flies you're going to miss the picnic." Through almost thirty-five years of church ministry, I realize how profound that was.

I still miss my father. I have enjoyed the picnic. I'm just sorry he had to leave early.

HEEEEERE'S JOHNNY!

Spending Time between Good Intentions and Missed Opportunities

I lost an old friend a couple of years ago. We first met in 1968, when I was a sophomore in high school. For those of you old enough to remember, the '60s were rather turbulent. In one decade, John and Robert Kennedy and Martin Luther King Jr. were assassinated, and Charles Whitman killed thirteen people on the University of Texas campus. There were shootings at Kent State University, and we were at war in Vietnam.

My friend and I hit it off immediately because with everything bad going on in the world, he could always make me laugh. Laughter is a good thing. We didn't really spend any time together on the weekends, only during the week. We ran in different circles. In fact, the only thing we had in common was a sense of humor.

Sometimes he cracked me up with just the expression on his face, a raised eyebrow, a smirk, or a deadpan straight face. Our friendship lasted for more than twenty-five years. Then, with only a short good-bye, he moved away in 1992. I never heard from him again, until January 2005. His name was Johnny Carson. We never really met, but I feel as though I've lost a friend. He did provide me with a lot of laughter.

One of my favorite episodes of *The Tonight Show* was from 1969. George Gobel was one of his guests. Johnny, George, Dean Martin, and Bob Hope were talking about military service, and George said that during World War II he was a fighter pilot trainer stationed in Oklahoma. They all laughed. George said, "Go ahead and laugh. I don't care. But if you think back, there was not one Japanese aircraft that got past Tulsa." To today's sophisticated audience, that probably would not be funny. Johnny, Dean, and Bob doubled over in laughter. I still think it's funny.

I never got the chance to thank Johnny for the laughter. Charles Dickens once said, "No person is useless in this world who lightens the burden of another." For me, Johnny Carson was a burden lightener. His passing has caused me to do some soul searching and ask some questions. Are there people around me who have lightened my burdens at one time or another by helping me or encouraging me? Have I ever thanked them? Have I ever lightened someone else's burden?

As Christians, I think part of our responsibility is to be burden lighteners wherever we go. I try to travel the road of good intentions, but too often I get stuck in the potholes of missed opportunities. Don't be like me. Stay away from the potholes. Do something that will lighten someone else's burden, and show someone appreciation for lightening yours. Anyone can cause a burden to be heavy, but it takes a special person to make it lighter.

62. Spending Time between Good Intentions . . .

As for me and my friend, we've gone our separate ways. That's OK. I have a lot of good memories. Every now and then I can even hear that old familiar voice from the past saying, "Heeeere's Johnny," . . . and I smile.

Stray Dogs, a Burning Bush, and One Inspiring Preacher

I love reading about the exploits of courageous dogs, especially those that have performed a miraculous feat by saving the life of a human being. Neither Molly, Tiny, nor Hershey, our Yorkshire terrier, has ever saved me from drowning, pulled me from a fire, or pushed me out of the path of an oncoming truck.

Tiny did deservedly bite our youth minister one time, and Molly, upon reaching her boiling point, will sometimes attack a fly. Hershey does not bark very well, but he does mess around on the computer. You might say his bark is worse than his byte. It seems their collective contribution to life has been playing, barking, sleeping, and eating—which, come to think of it, more than qualifies them to be a solid minister of music.

A man in Springdale, Arkansas, had his dog in the cab of his truck when he pulled up to an auto parts store. He ran into the store for an item and left the engine running with the truck in neutral. The dog got impatient and began running back and forth in the cab, eventually striking the gearshift, putting the truck in gear. The next thing the employees noticed was a truck coming through the front window with a dog behind the wheel. It may have been an accident, but that doggy in the window was expensive.

I was even more impressed by an article I clipped from a local newspaper. A three-year-old boy, dressed only in a T-shirt and shorts, wandered from his house and into the woods. Fortunately the family pet, a large dog named Samantha, stayed with him as he wandered away. Samantha was a stray the family had adopted several years earlier.

The boy wandered so far away he was gone overnight and in cold weather. During the night the dog nudged him beneath a bush, stayed close to him, and kept him warm. The next morning, Samantha helped lead him to one of the many search parties formed to look for him. Great story. Great dog.

God spoke to Moses through a burning bush. A little boy was saved by a stray dog. God spoke to me through a preacher whose soul burned with sadness. Dr. John Claypool was pastor of Broadway Baptist Church in Fort Worth, Texas, when I was at seminary in Fort Worth. I was hooked the first time I heard him preach.

I was a first-semester seminary student who only knew three people in the entire city. I was lonely. It wasn't like college. Dr. Claypool's preaching was that warm nudge I needed on a cold dark night. He took the chill off of a cold and wandering child. I tried to stay on his mailing list after I graduated from seminary, but I eventually lost contact with him.

Dr. Claypool died in September 2005. He used to close every

sermon with a benediction that talked about the goodness of God, the grace of God, and the love of God, and a reminder that we are continually being redeemed. I saw that expressed in the life and ministry of John Claypool. He was one inspiring preacher.

Where's Randolph Scott When We Need Him?

There is one figure in American history who stands out above all the rest as one of the greatest heroes of all time. Every male child growing up in the 1950s wanted to be this person. He could do no wrong and lived the most danger-filled and exciting life anyone ever imagined. He inspired bravery, chivalry, determination, commitment, and heady thoughts of good always winning out over evil. Of course, I'm talking about Mr. Potato Head.

When the newness of Mr. Potato Head wore off, though, we turned our attention to the cowboy of the Old West as our new hero. I remember running around the house being a cowboy, shooting bad guys, and dressed in the cowboy garb of hat, vest, boots, and a pair of six-guns. After a trip outside and hearing the lady next door scream, I remembered to add the all-important cowboy garb of blue jeans. I protected my neighborhood from bank robbers, and there wasn't a stagecoach in the county that got held up on my street.

When I wasn't driving out bank robbers, I was doing that other thing cowboys did: wiping stuff off the bottom of my boots before I went into the house. Once the neighborhood was safe and my boots were clean, I grew weary of the black hole of boredom I had entered and joined the cattle drive. I lived *Rawhide,* the television series from the 1950s. I was Gil Favor, trail boss; or Rowdy Yates, head dogie. I drew the line at being Wishbone, the cook.

Cowboys on the cattle drive had a tough life. They wore the same clothes every day, ate beans for supper, never had to clean their room, and only showered once a month. It was like going to college. After being with cows for a month, eating beans around the campfire, and rarely bathing, whenever they went into town their smell drove people away. This is where cowboys got the name "drovers." It was all fun, and I had a great time—until I started referring to my mother as Wishbone.

One of my favorite cowboy stars of the '50s was Randolph Scott. He appeared in more than forty Westerns from the 1930s to the early '60s, making his last one in 1962. I have several of them on tape. In fact, most of the movies I watch are from the 1930s to the 1960s. There was something about Randolph Scott that made a kid feel good about himself. I knew he wasn't going to get into a fight unless he was forced. If he did fight, I knew he would win. He fought on the side of the law and always tipped his hat to a lady. There's a novel idea for the new millennium.

Growing up, the only bad words I heard were at school. We didn't seem to need them to make a good movie. The so-called heroes in today's movies use language that would make a screen cowboy blush. And don't get me started on the music. I guess

I'm old-fashioned, but there is nothing wrong with smiling, using good language, and treating people with respect.

Randolph Scott and others are gone, but I am afraid we lost more than a few screen heroes. We have an entire generation of kids who haven't seen a movie without foul language or something being blown up. I don't play cowboys anymore or ride off with a cattle drive. I only think about it. Randolph Scott is gone, but the idea of him will always be with me.

God's Will ... Sometimes Our Won't

(Letter to Mom on June 11, 1986, after the resignation of my friend and pastor, Clyde Glazener, from Calvary Baptist Church in Little Rock, Arkansas)

Dear Mom,

Sorry I haven't written since the ski trip, but I've been busy posing for ski posters and autographing fences. Anyway, I need to talk to someone and I know I can always talk to you.

Remember when I was about nineteen or twenty and I asked you where babies came from and you told me about the stork and Federal Express? Well, I'm confused again, but not about that. My pastor resigned last week, and his main line of reasoning was that he felt it was "God's will." Why is my initial reaction to that negative? If someone dies an untimely death we are quick to say that it was God's will, and yet when someone moves to a new area of ministry we question it as being God's will. I don't understand why we usually associate God's will with tragedy instead of service.

Some preachers tell us it is God's will that every Christian prosper. Mom, have you seen my Subaru lately? Whatever happened to the good old days when God's will was expressed through burning bushes and whale bellies? Has God mellowed through the years, or does He speak more with that "still, small voice" we read about in His Word? Maybe that's the problem in understanding God's will. Maybe we need to spend more time reading God's Word and less time idolizing it.

Maybe I'm confused because I don't know whether to be mad at God for calling Clyde or mad at Clyde for listening to Him. What about that church in Arizona? Surely they deserve part of the blame. And what about me? What's going to happen to me when we get a new pastor? If it was God's will that Clyde leave, then why am I hurting so much? Shouldn't God's will for one person be the same for another? I don't know. Now I'm beginning to sound like people who claim to know the mind of Christ on everything.

Maybe I'm just selfish about the whole matter. What right do I have questioning how God deals with another individual? I've been concerned about myself all this time and have given very little thought to the anguish Clyde must have gone through in order to reach his decision. I feel very small. You know, Mom, I should be thanking God for allowing me to know Clyde and his family these last six years. They are wonderful people, and I guess I have just taken them for granted. Clyde has been great for our church, association, and state. If I were honest, I would have to say I'm happy for him and I know he's making the right decision. I know they'll love him in Arizona.

Thanks for listening, Mom, but there is one more thing. Remember when I was about ten years old and I was sick for a month after my best friend moved away, and you said that we seldom realize what a good thing we have until it's gone? Well, I'm beginning to get that same feeling again . . .

On the Wings of a Great Blue Heron

*(Written in July 1993, after the death of my friend and former super-
visor, Lawson Hatfield)*

I first met Lawson Hatfield on a hot September day in 1972 at
Ouachita Baptist University. His youngest son was my roommate,
and we shared a suite in our dormitory with two other guys from
Immanuel Baptist Church in Little Rock. I had transferred as a junior, and they were all freshmen. Therefore, I was wiser, much more
mature, and immediately became the spiritual leader. I was a calming
influence when they would come up with some childish pranks like
chasing a mysterious light on the railroad tracks or doing something
on campus that involved streaking.

As I got to know Lawson better, I realized he was a warm,
funny, compassionate man who loved his wife, Juanita, and his
children: two average sons, Jerry and Stephen, and a perfect daughter,

Gracie. He also loved his work at the Arkansas Baptist Convention and the Siloam Springs Baptist Assembly.

During my summers after college and during seminary he hired me to be the recreation director at the assembly. It was not until then that I came to understand the passion he felt for the camp he directed for so many years. He fervently led us in singing our camp song, "Siloam." He made movements like a bird and educated the campers on the great blue heron that frequented the valley.

He also warned them, "Don't *chonk* rocks." It became a catch-phrase at camp for the 1970s and 1980s. After graduation from seminary, I became his associate in the Sunday school department of the Arkansas Baptist Convention, where I was in charge of explaining the phone system to him and interpreting the notes in the margin of his pocket calendar.

Because of my association with him, this has been a difficult column, made doubly difficult by my being at children's camp at Siloam Springs Baptist Assembly when I heard the news. Because of that, I couldn't even attend his funeral. In fact, most of this story was composed at various spots throughout the camp. But the main reason I am troubled is that I never took the time in recent years to tell Lawson how much I loved and appreciated him. I was just too busy. Shouldn't that be a sin? It doesn't excuse my negligence, but many of us are guilty. We take our friends and family for granted and assume they will always be around. We seem to have criticism and anger down to an art but never take the time to work on our love and appreciation.

On June 30, 1993, God moved Lawson into a mansion in heaven that probably overlooks a valley of beautiful walnut trees and has a gazebo in the backyard. If you listen really closely, you can hear a heavenly admonition about "chonking" angels . . . and off in the distance, down at the far end of the valley, you can hear the faint cry of a solitary blue heron. It is very peaceful. God and Lawson are talking . . . and God can't help but smile.

"*Oh, next to my home, I love you, Siloam . . .*" and I love you, too, Lawson.

Walking through Life with a Loaded Goat

There are several incidents from the 1960s that should be included on a list of important events of the decade. A few that come to mind are the Cuban Missile Crisis; the assassinations of John F. Kennedy, Robert Kennedy, and Martin Luther King Jr.; the Vietnam War; and Neil Armstrong walking on the moon.

There was something else that happened during the 1960s. It was not so controversial (except when an attractive young lady tried to set up a manicure desk at Floyd's Barber Shop), never shock-filled (except when Aunt Bea drank some elixir), and seldom generated negative thoughts (unless Ernest T. Bass came to town). It was the *Andy Griffith Show,* set in the fictional town of Mayberry, North Carolina.

Mayberry wasn't really a town; it was a community in its truest sense. The people cared about each other. The stories revolved around a handful of townspeople with names like Andy, Aunt

Bea, Opie, Helen, Thelma Lou, Floyd, Otis, Gomer, and Ernest T. Bass. But the most unforgettable character was Barney Fife, perfectly portrayed by Don Knotts, who died on February 24, 2006. For me, watching the show was and is "therapettic," (*therapeutic,* if you don't know Barney).

Barney Fife was a nervous deputy who let his mouth get him into trouble. In several episodes Barney started out as the goat but ended up the hero. That's what community does. One man's weakness is another man's strength. It changes goats into heroes.

In one episode, Barney's ego caused Andy to be on trial. Eventually Barney's mouth saved the day. He told the trial lawyer that Andy was more than a sheriff to the people of Mayberry; he was their friend. He closed his speech with these words that Andy had tried to teach him for years: "When you're dealing with people, you do a whole lot better if you go not so much by the book, but by the heart." Wonderful words of community.

If Mayberry was nothing else, it was a reminder to me that church, in its truest sense, is like a community. It is a group of people who care about each other and who want to reach out in love to those around them. They don't spread gossip when a person faces difficult times. They care more about the person with the problem than they do the problem of the person.

One of my favorite episodes was "The Loaded Goat." A goat gets loose in Mayberry, eats several sticks of dynamite, and presents a real danger to the concerned citizens. In theory, the goat could explode at any time. The only thing that keeps him calm is Barney's harmonica playing. The final scene of the episode has Andy leading the goat out of town with Barney playing a soothing tune on the harmonica.

We all walk through life with a loaded goat. Circumstances

could blow up in our face at any time. In a community of believers, we have friends who will be there for us, to help prevent us from being consumed by circumstances. They have the gift of budnipping. In a community of believers we don't have to walk alone.

Thank you, Barney, for many wonderful memories . . . especially of how to treat people with heart and how to walk through life with a loaded goat.

lesson 68

Shadows Were Made for Tears

The willingness with which our young people are likely to serve in any war, no matter how justified, shall be directly proportional to how they perceive the veterans of earlier wars were treated and appreciated by their nation.

—George Washington

His grave is nondescript. It looks like any one of a thousand others around him. His grave site, near the amphitheater, is the second most visited grave in Arlington Cemetery . . . behind that of John F. Kennedy. Before he reached his twenty-first birthday, he had become the most decorated combat soldier of World War II. His name was Audie Murphy. He received his Medal of Honor for action near Holtzwihr, France, in 1944.

He returned home from the war a hero, making the cover of *Life* magazine in July 1945. He had parades and accolades from the country he loved, and he went on to become one of the biggest movie stars of the 1950s. He suffered from posttraumatic stress disorder, and he cried through the torment of losing close friends in battle. He died, unherolike, in a plane crash outside of Roanoke, Virginia, in 1971.

Another soldier's grave, like Audie Murphy's, is also nondescript. It looks like any one of a thousand others around him. His grave site, in the area of the amphitheater near the Tomb of the Unknown Soldier, is seldom visited. Hardly anyone knows who he was. After two tours of duty and by the time he was twenty-nine years old, he had become the most decorated combat soldier of the Vietnam War. His total of thirty-seven medals was more than Audie Murphy and Alvin York combined. His name was Joe Hooper. He received his Medal of Honor for action near Hue, Republic of Vietnam, in 1968.

He returned home from the war—alone and forgotten. The covers of magazines eluded him. There were no parades, no accolades from the country he loved, only shouts of "Baby killer!" He struggled with posttraumatic stress disorder and cried through the torment of losing close friends in battle. He died, unherolike, from a cerebral hemorrhage in a motel room in Louisville, Kentucky, in 1979.

The gravestones of Audie Murphy and Joe Hooper may be small and nondescript, but I have stood in their giant shadows. I was moved and felt unworthy trying to imagine what they experienced during and after the war. The ones who survive the rain of bombs and bullets in wartime always seem to struggle through the reign of sorrow and suffering in peacetime. I consider them heroes.

I am thankful for Audie Murphy, Joe Hooper, and all of our veterans, past and present. Veterans Day is an opportunity to express our thankfulness. It is a time to stand in the shadow of that eighty-year-old man who still walks with a limp or that nineteen-year-old boy fighting on foreign soil today and take a moment to reflect on our freedom. They deserve our respect, our gratitude, our remembering. God help us all if we never feel the shadow.

lesson 69

Ode to the Little Preacher

(Written in December 2000, after my pastor, Dr. Jimmy Gentry, announced he was moving to Carrollton Baptist Church in Carrollton, Georgia)

You came to us five years ago, and all we could do was stare;
We couldn't take our eyes off of you; everything moved but
    your hair.
Your ministry began; it was exciting and the church felt very
    lucky,
Until you made your first mistake: you said you hated Kentucky.

We had your reception in a pasture; people were full of smiles.
Instead of a welcome on carpet, you spent two hours dodging
    piles.
The summer passed, and you saw the beauty of a Tennessee fall;

69. Ode to the Little Preacher

Then you did it again: you said you didn't care for the Vols.

I remember the fun times, like when you baptized Jantzen
    Pendley;
As you stepped into the water, you both seemed so friendly.
Something was wrong; the temperature of the water made you
    dance.
When Jantzen shouted, we knew you had ice water in your
    pants.

We fix things slowly around here; it doesn't take long to see.
The problem with the baptistery began in 1973.
The roof is rather leaky, but we don't want to try anything
    new;
To fix a leak in our sanctuary, we just put another pot on
    the pew.

The problems with our outdated kitchen have nothing to
    do with you;
But at your reception this Sunday, I think we'll have barbecue.
We've shared a lot of meals; I've seen you eat until I hurt.
Even with all of that food inside, you're still a scrawny little
    squirt.

You listened to God, and you challenged us to live by the
    Word.
We did a few things differently, but we always said, "Jesus is
    Lord!"
You involved children in worship, and the reaction was not
    always mild;

You said to be truly Christlike, we simply need the faith of a
child.

It can be stressful serving on a staff; some people can be
sinister.
They ask you to give and give, but who ministers to the
minister?
We had a few laughs, we shed a few tears; you truly are a
brother.
In sharing some tough times, I guess we ministered to each
other.

We've had a great relationship, but I know we now must part;
You have Georgia on your mind, but keep Springfield in your
heart.
You were there at my mother's funeral, in all of that beautiful
snow;
Because of emotional memories like that, it is hard to let you go.

As you leave I see your sadness, and yet I see some jubilation;
Or, as the Temptations sang, maybe it's "Just My
Imagination."
Some have an agenda for the new pastor, before you leave our
sod;
I wish they'd put politics aside for a change, and leave it up to
God.

When you talk to your new friends, it will certainly be no
disgrace.
You were a part of us; you served God in this wonderful place.

69. Ode to the Little Preacher

Most of us here have loved you; we know you don't have
   horns.
Look on us with fondness; remember the roses . . . not the
   thorns.

Everyone has an idea of what they want the new pastor to be,
But I know the most popular characteristic, so leave it up to
   me.
If we ever get a search committee, I will sincerely pray from
   the heart,
"Lord, I don't care where he's from, just don't let him be so
   short."

lesson 70

A Personal Interpretation of the Twenty-Third Psalm

(I wrote this upon my mother's death and read it at her funeral on January 27, 2000, at Pulaski Heights Baptist Church in Little Rock, Arkansas.)

1. The Lord is my Guide and Comforter; in the midst of uncomfortable situations, I do not lack what I need to get through them. When I would go astray and forget to ask for guidance, my mother would gently remind me that I have everything I need.

2. Because so much of my emotional energy is spent in the rough waters of ministry and parenthood, He makes me take a rest now and then in the green pastures of a mother's embrace and guides me to the still waters of a mother's love

. . . and there are plenty. Sometimes I get so busy in life that I forget to provide my children the same green pastures and still waters.

3. For it is in the still waters where He does his best restoration job on my soul. It is only there that I listen to His charge about taking the right path. He makes me realize that, like my mother, I must continually be a positive role model for the people around me. I can accomplish that by letting Him lead me on the right path. It is for His sake, not mine.

4. Even though I walk through the valley of the shadow of church potluck dinners, long business meetings, and endless committee meetings, there is nothing left to fear . . . except possibly a deacons' meeting, but even in those dark times He is with me. His words, His love, and the prayers of my mother—they comfort me.

5. He is with me in the presence of those who do not agree with me and do not mind sharing endless words of discouragement. Sometimes it is a constant barrage. My head was once anointed with hair, but it only served to soak up criticism and keep in negative thoughts. Now I try to let criticism bounce off and allow the negative thoughts about people to be replaced with positive ones. It reminds me that I need to encourage people, not discourage them. My mother did just that. When I think of her example, my heart overflows.

6. There have been downtimes, and I know there will be more; but I know He will be with me bringing goodness, lovingkindness, and fond memories of my mother that will follow

me all the days of my life. She has left a legacy of goodness, kindness, and love that I will never forget, as long as I live. She has moved . . . and will live in the house of the Lord forever.

Chapter 8:
The Christian Life Is a Walk in the Park and I Just Stepped in Something

Lessons on Christian Growth

Eaters, Readers, or Doers of the Word?

A lthough Francis Bacon had the perfect last name for a farmer, he was a philosopher. He is credited with the following quote: "Some books are to be tasted, others to be swallowed, and some are to be chewed and digested." I mention this only because according to a recent news story someone took him literally.

Menelik II, emperor of Ethiopia from 1889–1913, believed there was power in the Scriptures . . . literally. Whenever he got sick, he ate a few pages. In 1913, he suffered a stroke. Thinking he needed an extra dose, he consumed the first two chapters of 1 Kings. He died instantly of intestinal complications. You might say he bit off more than he could chew. We do that sometimes with the Bible.

Man seems to have a way of getting into some difficulty when he misuses or misquotes the Bible. "To thine own self be true" is a phrase usually attributed to the Bible. It's from Shakespeare's *Hamlet*. The following is a list of things you will never read in the Bible, but there is a message in most of them. Eve to Adam: "Honey, does this outfit make me look fat?" Noah to God: "Is this forty days going to have a purpose?" God to Satan: "Is that your final answer?"

God to Jonah: "Can you hear me now?" Pharaoh at the Red Sea: "Looky there, fellas! He's leaving the trail wide open!" Goliath to David: "Hey, squirt! What's that silly contraption you're swinging around your . . .?" A simpleminded guard on the walls of Jericho: "Hey, can you guys play any Louis Armstrong?" Lazarus: "Boys, I wouldn't worry about covering the entrance. I won't be here very long." The zebras to Noah: "Could we be seated away from the carnivores?"

Lot's wife: "You know, I don't have to turn all the way around to see. If I can just turn my head a little bit more to the right I can . . ." Mary to Joseph: "Honey, I know we talk about everything, but you might want to sit down for this next one." The biggest lion, to his friend in the den with Daniel: "You know, Hank, I think I'll just have a salad."

The stories mentioned above all have a common theme: God is in control. God had a purpose in assembling these Scriptures. Every story has a purpose. The Old Testament points people to God, anticipating the coming of the Messiah. The New Testament points people to God, through the story of God's Son, Jesus, the Messiah, anticipating eternity.

We don't need to fight over the Bible, take away from it, or add to it. We know what we are to do. We are to take God's Word, apply it to our lives, and tell other people about it. If we have truly digested God's Word, our actions will reflect it.

Too many spiritually starving and sick people may be dying because of our complications with the Scriptures. In this wonderful banquet of life God has provided for us, the Scriptures were made for carrying out, not dining in.

Does Your Spiritual Exercise Include Talking in Place and Running from God?

If we were playing the game show *Jeopardy*, the answer would be "The person in the Bible who smelled most like the inside of a fish." Your question could be, "Who was John the Baptist?" and you would be close. He did have a strange diet. Of course, the correct question would be, "Who was Jonah?" We know the story, but let's refresh our memories.

God had a job for Jonah to do and told him to go to Nineveh. Jonah, in one of his more brain-impaired moments, thought he could run from God and fled in the opposite direction toward Tarshishkabob but only got as far as Tarshish. He booked passage on a ship with some offbeat sailors and headed across the sea. But the Lord called Congress together and blew a strong wind that tossed the tiny ship to and fro. Judging from the hair styles of the time, it was mostly fro. It extended the original charter for more than just a simple three-hour tour. The fun-loving sailors, particularly the Professor and Mary Ann, blamed Jonah for the storm and told him to go jump in the lake . . . so he did.

With the instrumental theme from *Jaws* blaring in the background, a large fish (obviously not in school) swam by, mistook Jonah for a plastic worm, and swallowed him. With the exception of spending a few days in Miami, I have never experienced anything like living inside of a fish, although I did sit by a large, burly man in the theater one time who smelled like he could have actually been Charlie the Tuna.

The Bible never tells us what Jonah ate, but we have to assume he was surrounded by fast food. No lights, no phones, no motorcars, not a single luxury, but he did spend time in prayer. After three days, God said something to the fish. Then the fish, after first making sure its mother wasn't around, gave out a loud belch that would have made any church softball team proud, and Jonah landed on the beach. The fish looked extremely relieved; said, "Pardon me!"; and swam away.

How often do we find ourselves doing the same thing? Oh, not the indigestion but the running from God part. For some, it's as if we're training for an Olympic event as we continually run from God when He has something for us to do. The only difference between us and Jonah is his experience is recorded in the Bible for everyone to read.

We probably are in no danger of being swallowed by a literal whale, unless we fall in at Sea World, but if we run from God we will be just as miserable. The further we get from God, the darker it becomes. You don't have to be inside of a whale to experience whale-belly darkness.

Is God asking you to do something for His kingdom today,

this week, this month, this year? Stop running. Slow down. Stop talking. Listen to God. How about a not-so-biblical but thought-provoking moral of the story? If we are going to argue with God, we must remember it is only one small step from debate . . . to debait.

Depending on the Song,
Even a Monotone Can Sing in God's Choir

pinions are like rude cousins. Almost everybody has one, they can appear out of nowhere, and sometimes they just stink. I read an article in a tabloid newspaper. It was not about a hockey-playing marmoset giving birth to a moose, Amelia Earhart being alive and working as a welcome lady at a Wal-Mart in Wisconsin, or a walrus eating sushi with chopsticks in a dry Kansas creek bed and wearing an "I'm with stupid" T-shirt while listening to the Four Seasons's "Working My Way Back to You."

No, this article was strange. It concerned a former FBI agent who wrote a book about John F. Kennedy's assassination. His opinion was that during the operation to save the president's life, surgeons discovered a tiny implant in his brain, placed there by either some fun-loving Republicans or extraterrestrials. This theory in itself should explain why the man is a *former* agent.

I have some real concerns and questions that need to be answered. Why would Amelia Earhart intentionally choose Wisconsin? What is a walrus doing in Kansas when he could have been at Disney World? Why are Republicans having fun? Why was it so easy to compare Republicans to extraterrestrials? These have not been answered to my satisfaction, but there is even a more horrific thought. If aliens could place implants in the president's brain, how much easier would it be to get to that person sitting in your recliner with a remote control and the brain of a pickle?

Alien intrusion could explain things like the popularity of alternative meat products, basketball shoes that cost the same as my first car, the term *gross national product* and how it relates to movie-theater floors, and where some articles of clothing go after they enter the dryer—what scientists refer to as the Bermuda Shorts Triangle.

The idea of brain implants is an intriguing one. With a brain implant, we could get teenagers to accept the concept that parents actually have sense. We could get people to be more loving and forgiving, in a Jesus sort of way. But let's not use the brain. Down a little lower. The tongue? Not bad. Some people could use a revised tongue. I'd much rather see Christians with a chip on their tongue rather than their shoulder. But it's still not the best.

Has to be the heart. What better place for an implant, or even a transplant. And God thought of it long before the aliens. Like the old hymn says, "In the heart He implanteth a song." God is in the implanting business. He has implanted a song in our hearts, and He has implanted us where He needs us. For God's choir to be effective, we must sing the song where we are. God needs all kinds and all parts.

Are you singing . . . or are you just mouthing the words?

Cinnamon Cholesterolls and Bumpy Tricycle Rides

In my ongoing battle with cholesterol and lining my arteries with bacon, I often borrow and alter the words of naval officer Olive Perry at the Battle of Erie in 1813: "I have met the enemy, and it is cheese." It may not be happening to you, but there are broken-down church buses full of cholesterol on the interstate, dodging the orange cones, trying to enter my body through the three major foods: Krispy Kreme donuts, Mexican food, and most of your basic cow-originated products. They seem to be succeeding. The only number higher than my cholesterol level is my average golf score.

Let me explain cholesterol in a way even our readers in South Carolina will understand. Cholesterol is a soft, waxy substance found in the bloodstream, not to be confused with the soft, waxy substance found in many dishes at potluck dinners. Like preachers and lawyers, cholesterol comes in two forms—good and bad. Good cholesterol comes from Arkansas, and bad cholesterol enters our body through Memphis. Something called triglycerides are involved, but they don't create a problem unless the tires go flat or the training wheels fall off.

Cholesterol by itself is not bad. The biggest problem with cholesterol and professional wrestlers is fat. Fat is evil and enters our bodies through desserts, fried foods, excess committee meetings, and animal organ meat. Animal piano meats are acceptable, although it is difficult to find a good piano tuna.

There are four main groups of fats. Saturated fats are in any foods that have taste. Monosaturated fats are fats that are tone deaf. These are prominent in church choir members who cook with peanut oil. Stereosaturated fats are those fats that linger after listening to too many Barry Manilow records. Polyunsaturated Fats is Minnesota's sister.

The best way to control fat and cholesterol is to quit going to committee meetings or sew your lips together. If you like to gossip and this is not convenient, then eat high-fiber foods like hay, insects, paper sacks, and medical journals. Animals are OK to eat if you avoid the meat and just eat the hair, teeth, and toenails.

It should be obvious we need to care of our bodies, especially the heart. We need to start young with a proper diet and continue through the adult years. It takes discipline in watching what we eat and exercising properly. Just as obvious for the Christian should be the fact that we need to take care of our spiritual body. Psalm 119:70 says, "Their heart [the proud] is as fat as grease, but I delight in Your law" (NKJV).

Want to get rid of unwanted spiritual fat like complacency, arrogance, and negative attitudes? Try a steady diet of prayer, Bible study, worship, fellowship, and ministry. It may be a bumpy ride, but exercise your heart. Do the things Jesus did. Get your heart in shape, because life, whether physical or spiritual, always seems to boil down to a heart thing.

Do Churches Last Longer When Built on a Cross Rather Than Platform Heels?

If it had not been next to the larger headline that said, "Elvis Photographed While Picking a Corn off Bigfoot," I would have been more shocked. The smaller headline said, "Bell-Bottom Pants Back in Style." I hadn't been that terrified since I tried to renew my driver's license. For those of you who were never inoculated against bell-bottoms, let me explain them to you. They were so big at the bottom that you could roll a basketball up the pants leg without it ever touching the side of the pants.

When starched, they could be draped over a pole and shelter a family of ten. If you got them wet on a rainy day, any forward movement would require a forklift. If they got wet during an ice storm, you could use them to ram maiden-voyage passenger ships. The best part was wearing them on a windy day in Amarillo. If the wind caught you just right, you could end up in Tulsa.

There was more to this fashion nightmare. No pair of bell-bottoms was complete without platform shoes. If life were a pond and bell-bottoms were the scum, platform shoes would be the carp. Platform shoes were designed by someone who had either lost all of his important chromosomes or had peas for brains. Like the California Redwood, you could drive trucks through the heels.

I had a pair of platform shoes in college with secret compartments where I kept a quadraphonic music system, a navy blue bowtie, a pair of plaid pants, a navy blue vest sweater, and a white dress shirt with a collar big enough to land small planes. That was my outfit for my singing group . . . or posing for a reproduction of *The Little Dutch Boy.* Thankfully, bell-bottoms and platform shoes were only fly-by-night fads. Dressed like that, I certainly did not want to fly in the daytime.

Unfortunately, churches are sometimes guilty of succumbing to whatever is popular, fashionable, and appealing in their efforts to reach people. People need protein and vitamins, but the church offers them Twinkies. We expound on programs and policies when we should be exhorting repentance and relationship. Whether they are boomers (born 1946–64), busters (children of the boomers), or tasters (my term for people who want to just get close enough to church to catch the drippings), they still respond to love, the kind exemplified by Christ on the cross.

Therefore, to keep people who come in the front door from going out the back, we must involve them through the ministry of small groups and Sunday school. Sunday school is nothing new, but it is how we care for people.

Are you as a teacher, leader, member, or facilitator doing your share? An army of committed Christians can accomplish more for the kingdom of God than a handful of preachers. Remember, Custer would have won his battle if all he had to do was fight the chiefs . . . unless his soldiers had been wearing platform heels.

The Wilderness Looms on the Horizon When Sacred Cows Become Golden Calves

Of all the characters in the Bible who did not get swallowed by a whale, I believe Moses is the leading candidate to win the "This-event-has-movie-potential-written-all-over-it" award. You remember his beginning. It was the best of times; it was the worst of times . . . for baby boys in Egypt. His parents, Amwayram (of the tribe of Levi, who later invented a swell pair of jeans) and Jochebed (from which we get the terms *Jochechair* and *Jochesofa*), hid him in a basket among the bulrushes along the Nile River. No one has ever actually seen a bulrush. They usually stay in the pasture and move very slowly, unless it is during bulrush-hour traffic.

He was then discovered by a princess and raised in the court of Pharaoh. (Pharaoh is remembered for his most famous statement, "A typo! Well, that certainly would explain Moses's preoccupation with those ten plaques.") Moses eventually killed an Egyptian soldier and fled to Idaho, where he was not heard from for years.

Moses was amazing. He picked up a stick and changed it into a snake, talked to a burning bush, led a bunch of cranky people through the wilderness for forty years, parted the Red Sea without a comb, and defeated the Amallekites—a group of ferocious fighters who hung out in Egyptian shopping centers. In later life he had two sons, Charlton Eliezer and Heston Gershom.

His greatest accomplishment (besides a really cool Cecil B. De-Mille movie) was climbing Mount Sighnigh (pronounced "Sinai," and sometimes called Mount Horeb because of its close proximity to Mount Hoyank). He came down with the Eleven Commandments. Some oral traditions tell us there were originally eleven, but Moses got mad at the Israelites and broke the first one, which said, "Thou shalt not break these tablets."

He was mad at the Israelites for their lack of faith, their stubbornness, their impatience, and ultimately their worship of something other than God—a crudely constructed golden calf. Moses smashed it into powder and had them drink the dust.

We also have our golden calves, but they are subtler, because they sometimes begin as sacred cows. A sacred cow is anything that cannot be criticized or changed. It may be a building, a classroom, a tradition, a picture of Jesus, or something else. If it becomes greater than God, we might as well live according to the Nine Commandments. Forget the one about idols.

Do you have a sacred cow? Can you prevent it from becoming a golden calf? One of the problems churches face today is there are too many sacred cows on the verge of becoming golden calves—and our churches, like the people of Israel, could choke on the resulting dust.

Reaching People in the State of New Hamster

Even for those of you who do not have teenagers in your household, we live in a strange and confusing world. It is evident by the invention of hamsters and computers. I survived my initial foray into hamsterology only because I armed myself with enough colored plastic tubes to build a second tunnel under the English Channel . . . which runs parallel to the Discovery Channel. Besides providing a home, the tubes gave the hamster a snack to gnaw on at two in the morning. Gnawing is easy because he has large teeth called incisors, which comes from a Latin word meaning, "Even duct tape cannot prevent me from eating through these tasty plastic tubes."

The word *hamster* comes from the German word *hamstern*, which means "to hoard," from which we get the word *accountant*. The most popular type of hamster for a children's pet is the dwarf hamster, easily recognizable because they are always Bashful,

Sleepy, or Grumpy. For parents, the most popular type of hamster is the dead hamster, easily recognizable because it has ceased gnawing. Hamsters, like many people walking on public beaches, have expandable cheek pouches and generally do not mix well with other hamsters.

The jury is still out on whether or not I will survive computers. I gave up trying to learn computer terminology once I discovered *megabyte* wasn't a beaverlike dental problem. I miss the good old days when *fiber optics* was a health-food cereal containing eye parts, a *footnote* was a cheat sheet for a test when your hands and arms got full, *spreadsheet* was part of making up your bed, *justified* involved faith and Martin Luther, and *hyperlink* was a sausage on NoDoz.

I remember when *opening windows* involved fresh air, the *Italics* were great cooks, a *control panel* was something my mother wore, a *blinking cursor* was a sailor with nervous eyes, a *sixteen-inch monitor* was a really short guy in the hallway at school, and *align bottom* was the first step in changing a diaper.

With hamsters having babies every twenty-eight days and technology reproducing computers almost as often, it would be easy to get frustrated amid the confusion. Unfortunately, words like *confusion* and *frustration* have now entered the vocabulary of the church. Religious scandals are front-page news, different groups boycott particular religious gatherings, and we battle over worship styles.

Although it has been disguised, disregarded, and even dishonored, one thing has remained constant throughout the ages—the mission of the church. The church still exists for those who are sick, not those who are well. The church is here to reach people; and no matter in which spiritual state a person may find himself, God has a place for him in His church. Jesus said, "Healthy people don't need a doctor—sick people do" (Mark 2:17 NLT). In today's terms . . . the Doctor is in, and the appointment book is wide open.

lesson 78

When Jumping to Conclusions Becomes an Olympic Event

U nless you have spent the last few years inside a cave or talking with someone who still doesn't believe the Mets won the '69 World Series, you are aware of the Olympics. The opening ceremony is always one of the highlights, the other being listening to the announcers try to pronounce the foreign names of the athletes born without vowels.

I remember the Winter Olympics of 1998 in Nagano, Japan. (*Nagano* is a Japanese word that means "to rub a friend's head furiously with your knuckles." Our English equivalent is *noogie.*) It is during the opening ceremony that the host country, through majestic backgrounds, grandiose musical productions, and intricately woven themes, enlightens a worldwide television audience about its native culture. This would explain Nagano's squatting Sumo wrestlers. (*Sumo* is a Japanese word that means "bus-in-a-diaper.")

78. When Jumping to Conclusions Becomes an Olympic Event

With several thousand pounds of aplomb, the sumos paraded in and performed a religious ceremony of purifying the stadium before the games began. They did this by squatting, squinting, growling, and clapping—driving out the evil spirits. (It was very similar to the procedure my college fraternity followed in purifying our meeting place.) It was extremely confusing to the naked eye.

To the clothed eye, it would be like making the Japanese people watch preachers on American television during full-contact prayer time, which includes clapping, shouting, squinting, growling, and slapping people in the head. This ultimately drives out evil spirits. (It also would account for the many spectators leaving the service with flat foreheads and broken limbs, but completely healed of their nausea.) The main sumo in the ceremony was 6'7", weighed 480 pounds, and in his spare time provided shade for family reunions. To me the entire ceremony seemed like a bizarre aerobic/weight-loss experiment gone sour.

I wonder sometimes if what goes on in the Christian arena is confusing to the nonbeliever. Strange things do occur under the guise of religious activity. Slain animals are found in remote locations and attributed to a local cult as a blood sacrifice to God. Others use violence toward humans because they claim to have orders from God. It makes one wonder what in God's name is going on. There's the rub. God could do without much of what goes on "in His name."

We can point fingers at other religions and their questionable practices, but we need to be responsible for ourselves. We are to be representatives of Christ everywhere we go. We are to be in God's name, living out the Beatitudes and the fruit of the Spirit. We must not create confusion for the nonbeliever.

Unfortunately, for some of us the Beatitudes and the fruit of the Spirit seem to be hurdles rather than goals. In the worldwide arena of Christian living, I am glad living them is not an Olympic event. I fear I would never make the team. Would you?

Something Wicker This Way Comes

Part of being a dutiful husband is acknowledging the superiority of the female in all things, especially when it comes to picking out household furniture for its aesthetic value rather than its practicality. It works perfectly in my marriage because I was born without the furniture-placement chromosome. For example, my idea of nice bookshelves is a board and some cinder blocks.

My impairment is not limited to furniture. I suffer from a similar malady when it involves hanging pictures. When hanging pictures, I have but one requirement: whether I can see all of the dogs playing poker in one glance. None of that really matters right now because there is an evil trend lurking underneath the surface of seemingly innocent home design and décor. It is a concept so heinous, barbaric, and wicked it may become the subject of a new reality television show. Yes, I'm talking about inflatable furniture.

If you have preschoolers or cats in your house, do not let them read any further.

This furniture has such wildly bright colors it looks like you are about to sit on a pile of Jell-O. I know what you are thinking: *This had to originate in California.* Wrong. This time they are innocent. One of the main U.S. distributors is in Illinois. Inflatable items now include sofas, chairs, pillows, clocks, tulips, and ottomans. (Speaking of Ottomans, if they had used this kind of furniture in the days of Alexander's empire, would they have referred to him as Alexander the Inflated?)

Call me old-fashioned, but I draw the line at blow-up plastic furniture . . . well, unless it has a drink holder. I have enough trouble trying to fit my body onto one of those water rafts in the pool without having to wrestle with one in the living room. Besides that, it makes funny noises when you rub it the wrong way. You get ten people in your den trying to get out of those breath traps at the same time, and it would sound like the tuba section of a marching band. I don't want to sit on any piece of furniture that when I make contact it sounds like someone blew a tuba.

It takes all kinds, doesn't it? Look at your own house and see how many different styles of furniture are there. They are all unique, and each one has its own function. Everything from bentwood to cherry wood, to wicker, and yes—even blow-up plastic furniture. That's exactly the way it is in God's house. Each person is different, each with a different function, some with inflated opinions of themselves and some just full of hot air, but all coming together under the motif of Christianity. We all need each other to make God's house what He would have it to be.

One more thing. Just as the plastic furniture must be filled with air to serve its purpose, so we must be filled with the breath of God to fulfill ours. Acts 1:8 says, "You will receive power when the Holy Spirit comes on you." If we are filled with anything else, we are powerless . . . and headed for deflation.

Best Performance by a Christian in a Supporting Role Is . . .

Over the years I have discovered three events in life that test our patience and seem to go on forever (four, if you count watching NASCAR drivers doing commercials). They are a twelve-hour camp-bound bus ride involving singing children, with at least one who is carsick and one who constantly seems to be needing a trip down porcelain lane; the five-hour part of the dance recital *after* your daughter performs; and the Academy Awards presentation on television.

The telecast usually comes to a merciful end after about three hours, equal to one teenager's conversation on the telephone. It is the best night of the year to see $25,000 designer gowns, many of which contain barely enough material to cover a poodle. Considering a few of the hair styles I saw, some of the gowns might have been covering a poodle.

I quit going to movies when John Wayne died. When our children were younger, they dragged us to movies that involved bizarre cartoon characters, talking animals, and communication at its lowest form. It would have been cheaper just to take them to a staff meeting at church. Occasionally, like at every appearance of Halley's Comet, I will agree to go with Beverly to see some icky love story. I prefer the light classics, such as *Abbot and Costello Meet the Wolf Man,* or *The Three Stooges Go to Mars.* Of course, those kinds of movies do not win many Oscars.

The movies that win the accolades cause the audience to reach deep inside themselves and thrust open a heretofore unopened door to the dark side of terror, forcing the viewer to take his unsuspecting heart on an excruciatingly painful roller-coaster ride of gut-wrenching emotions, but ultimately showing the triumph of the human spirit under the most adverse conditions known to mankind. Sort of like being a schoolteacher at the elementary level.

Funny thing about the Oscar nominations. Everyone knows the actors and directors, but hardly anyone knows the production crew, without whom the movie could not have been made. Every movie has a "gaffer," and I don't even know what that is. It works that way in church. Everyone knows the staff, deacons, Sunday school teachers, and musicians, but what of the people who labor in children's choirs, missions groups, committees, or other volunteer areas? No church could function without them.

What of the people who take the time to call, write, or in some other way encourage the ones listed above? Not a bad ministry. Wonderfully heartfelt performance in a supporting role. There are no awards for service, but everyone likes to be loved, appreciated, and encouraged. Barnabas modeled it. He probably made Paul a better teacher. If there were a recognition, it could be called the Barnabas Award. Have you done anything lately to be nominated? Don't worry. There is no such award . . . at least not on earth.

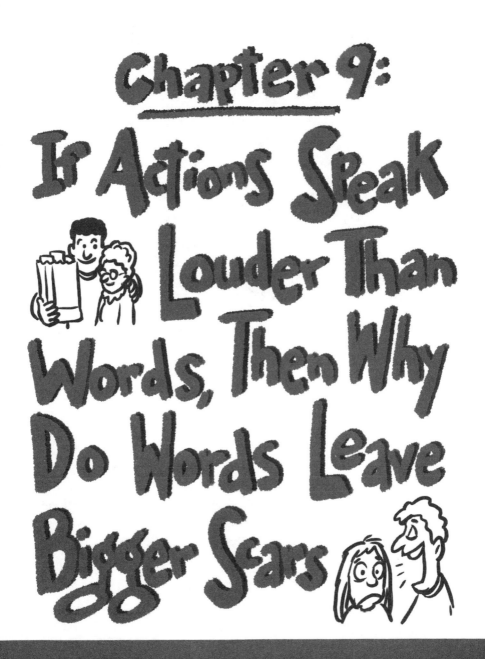

Chapter 9:
If Actions Speak Louder Than Words, Then Why Do Words Leave Bigger Scars

Lessons on the Power of Words

Can They Know We Are Christians by Our Words?

try not to think of my seminary days in Fort Worth, Texas. I still have nightmarish remembrances of smiley-faced ministerial students wandering through campus, lugging their forty-pound briefcases around like weapons of war. With a semi-holy aura and silent stare, they looked like *Twilight Zone* episodes waiting to happen. They gave the phrase "lost in space" a whole new meaning. I tried to avoid them but would occasionally come in contact with them long enough to overhear some of their conversations.

One of them haughtily asked me, "What do you think about the descent into hell?" I said, "I don't know. Is that anything like driving through West Memphis?" Most of them had no sense of humor, but they did enjoy using big theological words in their conversations. First preacher boy: "Could you believe that test on fissiparous Protestants and their splinter sects?" Second preacher boy, probably from Alabama: "No. Growing up in my house, we couldn't even talk about sects."

81. Can They Know We Are Christians by Our Words?

I did some research and found some legitimate theological words that could be very confusing if misunderstood. *Absolution*—a chemical mixture for soothing aching stomach muscles during long sermons. *Clergy*—the eighth dwarf, usually mentioned immediately following Sleepy and Dopey. *Cyril of Jerusalem*—another term for unclean breakfast food. *Dogma*—usually seen chasing cats with Dogpa. *Infallible*—a person who never trips over his own words. *Liturgical*—as in "I ate too many tacos with shrimp sauce and had to liturgical." *Opus Dei*—Andy Griffith's seldom-mentioned Latin son. *Paradox*—two MDs standing next to each other. *Proselyte*—a low-calorie prosel. *Pyrrhonism*—the process during which a swarm of deacons devours a fully mature adult preacher, with briefcase, in less than ten seconds. *Sacramentarians*—people from Sacramento. *Temptations*—a great '60s singing group. *Vatican*—the opposite of *Vatican't*.

Words can be so complicated, especially when they have more than five or six letters. When we talk about the salvation experience in church circles, we use words like *sanctified, justified, purified,* and *atonement.* Using these words outside the church would result in people looking at us as though we had two heads. That's why when sharing the gospel, we need to keep it simple. God loves us. Sin separates us from God. He sent His Son to die for us.

Words can also be confusing. Sometimes the words coming out of our mouths do not match our actions. It's difficult to talk to people about Jesus when they know our lifestyle is speaking a different language than our words. They may not understand complicated church words, but they do understand misleading actions. People will know we are Christians by our love . . . and hopefully, our words won't get in the way.

What a Friend We Have in Cheeses, When We Sleep in Heavenly Peas

*E*nglish is a funny language. It is even funnier when we see words that aren't really there or hear words that aren't actually spoken. Newspaper headlines and Baptists are particularly disturbing when it comes to words. This is not really news, but apparently a wild woman is causing havoc. Recent headlines have said, "Cuba Recovering As Michelle Hits Hard," or "Keys Evacuated As Michelle Nears." Clearly, this woman must be stopped.

Another one said, "330,000 Liberians Homeless from Strife." This is so sad. I feel especially bad for the Liberians, thinking they may be homeless because thousands of people like me have never paid their overdue book fees. The most frightening headline I've seen is "Buffalo Pumping Station Proposal Angers Residents." I agree with the angry residents. Why are we spending good money pumping Buffalo? Do we even know if they have gas? If they are full of gas, it will certainly be dangerous for them to be home on the range.

The other problem with our language is that so many words sound like something else and can be really confusing. I heard one news report about the anthrax problem at male-sorting centers. I didn't even know we had those. What is the latest on global worming? I know several people who would benefit from a good worming. Another troubling headline said, "New CEO Comes from Board." What is he, a termite? Maybe he just came from some splinter group.

I did some research and found some other words that are very disturbing. A simple word like *defer* can be confusing when used in this sentence: "When that otter hits the fan, defer will fly." Mustard gas is what happens to mustard when it eats too much cabbage. On a historical note, a soldier in the nineteenth century went deep into Florida, scouting ahead of his troop. He wanted to get delay of Deland. I don't know. Some days I just feel like putting on my butterfly formal and attending a mothball.

It is easy to see how words can be confusing. It makes me wonder why we are so careless and hurtful with them. Listen to Jesus's words from Matthew 12:35: "A good person produces good words from a good heart, and an evil person produces evil words from an evil heart" (NLT).

Good answer. Jesus was full of them. When we use words carelessly, it could lead someone to think we are not full of Jesus. We must be careful in what we say and what we think we hear. We have a friend in Jesus, and we sleep in heavenly peace. Careless words are cruel and divisive, not encouraging and unifying. Remember . . . it's not the piecemakers who are blessed.

Splinters in the Hands of an Angry God

Unless you live in *Mister Rogers' Neighborhood,* you have experienced anger at one time or another, especially if you have played church-league basketball. A few things that irritate me are people who wait until they get to the drive-through window at the bank before they begin filling out their deposit slip, people who drive too close to my rear bumper, and servers at the fast-food drive-through window who don't include stir sticks when I order cream and sugar with my coffee.

Other opportune times to get angry are children's soccer matches, Little League baseball games, and church business meetings where they decide whether to use cans or bottles in the Coke machine. Another great moment is when you take your car to the mechanic and it won't make "the noise" . . . um, the car, not the mechanic. They make plenty of noises.

One of the best places to find anger is in the quiet solitude of a happy marriage when the innocent husband wants to play a simple round of golf and the overbearing wife has a maniacal insistence that he mow the grass, rake the leaves, and trim the weeds in the garden. A somber week goes by and that poor husband wants to go fishing, but his Attila the Hun–like wife insists that he do the laundry, paint the den, and repair the shower stall.

The patient husband waits for another week and wants to hang out harmlessly with the guys on Saturday, but his unsympathetic wife explodes into a rage, insisting he clean out the garage. Finally, the ever-vigilant and pitiful husband gives up and falls into the recliner for a long overdue nap. Instantly, his thorns-for-a-heart wife zooms into a ballistic, blood-vessel-popping rage, insisting he take out the garbage. It is a bad situation, but it is not permanent. In other words, anger is like the newlywed wife cooking the first meal for her faithful husband: you can't escape it . . . but you *can* get over it.

Something that really gets to me is rubbing my hand over a piece of wood and getting a splinter. It is painful and aggravates me to no end. But in a spiritual sense, we put God through the same thing, because every time He is forced to carry our cross, we give Him a splinter. And it has to hurt. Whenever we refuse to do what we know God wants us to do, or we try to go our own way without Him, we give Him a splinter . . . and you can almost hear a cry of pain from heaven.

We get upset over the silliest things, and all too often we forget that God probably gets angry with us over things that really matter. Do golden calves or ignored Ten Commandments ring any bells? The goal of every Christian should be that whenever God places His hands on our shoulders, He doesn't draw back with a splinter. I would much rather hear Him say, "Well done, good and faithful servant," instead of, "Ouch!"

If You Attach Fishing Lures to Your Tongue, Are You Waiting with Baited Breath?

There is something disturbingly appetite-damaging about driving up to the fast-food restaurant window and receiving a sack of food from someone with a ball bearing or fishing lure surgically attached to his or her nose. Unfortunately, the piercing rarely stops at the nose. There are very few contemporary, John Wayne–like Westerns where the cavalry rides in to save the fort from the marauding bad actors posing as Indians, and I now know why. If the movie were made today, the Indian chief would have to say, "White man speak with forked *and* pierced tongue."

Not that I walk around the mall inspecting tongues anymore, but you do not have to sit very long on the husband-unifying benches before actual humanlike beings parade by with earrings protruding from areas that once were occupied by lint, lobes, or saliva. Shish-kebabbing my tongue is not high on my list of priorities—unless it cures baldness. Pierced tongues are not the only obstacles we face in understanding the complexities of today's mouth. Did you know there are more than three hundred different types of bacteria inside your mouth? . . . three thousand if you recently ate at a truck stop. Except for the occasional germ that reaches us through Texas, most of the bad germs enter our bodies through the mouth—and like telemarketers, they stay forever . . . unless you floss.

As early preschoolers, we learn to put things in our mouths, except for peas. This continues until the teen years, when nothing enters the mouth unless it is shaped like a pizza or an earring, and on into the adult years, when the mouth seems to be particularly partial to feet. If you think this is not a problem, just look into the mouth of the next person you meet and see how devastating the carnage is from bacteria . . . and too many telemarketers.

Indians, Alice Cooper fans, and dentists are not the only people concerned about the mouth—or what comes out. From the time our children first begin talking, we parents carefully monitor their progress and sometimes correct their grammar or scold them for using a less-than-appropriate word in front of grandmother. We also teach them to use respectful words with all people. Too bad we are not as conscientious about adult mouths.

Some adults use the tongue to bait people into saying something they will regret later. Others see chastisement—the negative, piercing sound of their own voice—as a spiritual gift. My Bible disagrees. James 3:6 says the tongue is dangerous, "an evil power that dirties the rest of the body."

Sounds like a bacteria . . . but it can be treated. Psalm 119:11 says, "I have hidden your word in my heart, that I might not sin against you" (NLT). If we must do something with our mouth, let's do it according to Scripture. It is the only piercing our tongue will ever need.

237

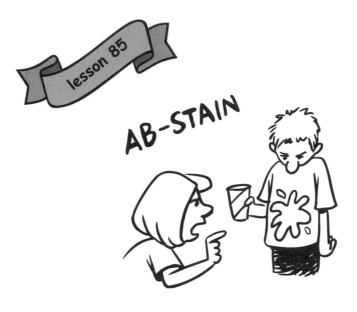

AB-STAIN

The Dangers of Expletive Constructions and Negative Adverbs

Words are a powerful invention. Except for communicating with rock musicians, they are a necessity. The great English poet William Wordsworth is credited with discovering all the important words in the English language . . . hence his last name. It used to be Wordsworthless. I still remember diagramming sentences in high-school English. I learned about *transitive verbs,* those verbs who have been overseas for an operation; *squinting modifiers,* modifiers who refuse to wear glasses; and *suspended compounds,* compounds who got in trouble at school.

I studied, but never conquered, *relative clauses* (Santa's cousins), *subordinate clauses* (elves), *passive gerunds* (senior adults who just really don't care), and *introductory paragraphs* (as in the statement, "Mr. Verb, meet Mr. Noun"). Being of puritanical background, I refused to study bare infinitives, expletive constructions, and dangling modifiers.

English is such a complicated language that we have to be careful how we use it. There are confusing words such as *accommodate*, someone who will go out with an accommo; *hasty pudding*, pudding that acts without thinking; *sacrifice fly*, an insect that enters a room first to test it for pesticides; and *scepter*, as in the statement, "She was so ugly no one loved her scepter mother." We also have words like *censure*, which means criticism or reproof in some parts of the South, as in, "Censure not picking up your dirty socks, I'm not cooking the possum"; and *nincompoop*, what you step in when you follow the nincoms in a parade.

There are misused words like *abstain*, a hard-to-remove spot on your stomach; *frayed*, an East Tennessee term in the statement, "Because of an earlier scare, he was frayed to walk through the cemetery"; and *decaffeinated*, which means to be without something, as used in the sentence, "Henry VIII and his wife Anne Boleyn argued over coffee so much that he cut off her head . . . she was decaffeinated."

Part of our responsibility as Christians is to communicate God's love to everyone we meet. In order to share effectively, we must not only master the English language but also be able to put our words together in a way that will glorify the Master. It is difficult if we have a habit of using abusive words. The writer of Proverbs says in 12:18, "Rash words are like sword thrusts, but the tongue of the wise brings healing" (NRSV).

Rash words do more than simply cause an itch. They make a person feel uncomfortable, unwanted, and unloved. Wouldn't it be great if we could take some of the great nouns of the New

Testament and make them verbs? Faith, hope, love, goodness, and patience all make wonderful religious nouns, but they don't mean a thing to unloved people without a conjunction to connect them . . . and that conjunction is the Cross. Because of the Cross, true Christianity will always be a verb.

Dodging Aunt Bea's Pickles and Digesting Jesus's Words

O ur topic for the week is pet peeves . . . as opposed to wild, undomesticated peeves. One of my pet peeves involves going to someone's house for dinner. It could be a friend, relative, or prison escapee. In West Virginia, the last two would probably be the same. For some reason, your hostess has felt compelled to try out a brand-new recipe on you with much pride. You bite into it, and it tastes like it was cooked inside a dead otter. Without a spittoon, there is no graceful way out.

This is an especially disturbing situation when the person trying out the new recipe is your wife. When she innocently asks how it was, you innocently but cunningly respond, "It's fine." Now, husbands, learn from this. Anytime your wife asks a question that requires passing judgment on her hair, clothing, or quality of cooking, "It's fine" is never an acceptable response. The end result will always be heartache, tears, bloodshed, and in some extreme cases the most heinous response of all . . . agonizing silence and a glare that could take down an armed caribou.

What can you say when you enter a friend's house for dinner and notice the mice waving a white flag and the family dog pointing to the kitchen and shaking his head? These are sure signs something evil is in the room. You must be careful to act correctly when confronted with less-than-conventional and convincingly contaminated culinary creations. However, you don't have to be alliterative.

A keen sense of smell at least gives a warning. If what is before you smells like someone gutted a possum, then you have a pretty good idea of how it will taste. Instead of nonthreatening comments like, "This is really a meal" or "You should not have gone to so much trouble," I want to hear things like, "Would you grab that casserole? It seems to be leaving" or "Mmm . . . that smell! Is dinner ready or did a whale explode?"

One episode of the *Andy Griffith Show* concerned Aunt Bea's homemade pickles ("kerosene cucumbers"). Andy and Barney tried to dispose of them by giving a jar to tourists on their way out of town. Ultimately, they realized the best approach was to learn to love them.

Some of the words of Jesus can be hard to swallow. We take seriously His words on prayer and sin (especially someone else's), but phrases such as "Be kind," "Love your enemies," and "Forgive one another" rarely make the journey from the pages of Scripture to our hearts. They get stuck somewhere along the journey.

Like a child at the dinner table, we play with the spiritual food Jesus gives us and choose only to digest the words we like, not necessarily the ones that are best for us. Jesus said, "People need more than bread for their life; they must feed on every word of God" (Matthew 4:4 NLT).

We must take all the words of Jesus to heart and practice them until they become a way of life. Only then will we be truly prepared to feast at His table.

Never Go into Battle Singing "March of the Wouldn't Soldiers"

I have never been big on the idea of making New Year's resolutions. Maybe it is because New Year's Day nearly always falls on January 1, and my mind is usually muddled because I have spent hours eating a football and watching black-eyed peas. By the time I have finished watching 117 football games in December and early January, my brain has all the retention capability of an unburped Tupperware dish.

I got frustrated several years ago when I tried to make a resolution concerning watching my hair and losing weight. In the confusion of transferring the idea to paper, I spent the whole year just watching my weight and losing hair. During the somewhat dubious course of my maturity, I have discovered there are countless others who suffer from a similar malady when it comes to New Year's resolutions.

Fictional history tells us that on January 1, 1846, Alfred Packer's New Year's resolution was to become a vegetarian. (Packer was one of the few people in the United States to be convicted of cannibalism.) Had he carried through with it, the Donner party's trek through the Sierra Nevada mountains during the winter of 1846–47 might have been, shall we say, less incr-edible? Years later, in 1967, that historical event was chronicled in the hit movie *Guess Who's Coming to Dinner?*

You may also recall that on January 1, 1892, Lizzie Borden made a resolution to give up her day job as a lumberjack. Had she fulfilled it, she would not have had such easy access to the tools of her trade and maybe her parents would not have been so deeply en-trenched on the cutting edge of late-nineteenth-century murder trial reform. Years later, Hollywood made a television movie about this experience . . . but many of the lesser parts were axed.

A favorite hymn in Christendom for more than 130 years has been "Onward, Christian Soldiers." It is much easier to sing the song than it is to live the words. It encourages us to accomplish God's task "with the cross of Jesus before us," when all too often our response to God's call is "I can't," "I won't," "I didn't," "I wouldn't." I am referring not to New Year's resolutions but to commitments we make to God, family, and friends.

Oh, that we would be more like Jesus. The following passages are examples of His promising words: "Today you will be with Me in Paradise" (Luke 23:43 NKJV); "I am the light of the world. He who follows Me shall not walk in darkness, but have the light of life" (John 8:12 NKJV); and "You will know the truth, and the truth will make you free" (John 8:32 TEV).

Ironic, isn't it? Some people say the greatest words in the Bible are the Ten Commandments, words probably etched in some form of stone; but for me, the greatest words in the Bible belong to Jesus . . . and those words are most assuredly carved in some form of *would*.

Relief for Any Allergy Can Be Found Right under Your Nose

I do not like to air dirty laundry (unless the wind is blowing toward Texas), but I have a problem with my family. They all have allergies. Many of you know what it is like to have your face swell up, have your nose turn three shades of red, and have so many lines in your eyes it is like looking at a road map of Boston. Well, for those of you with allergies, it is even worse.

David is so allergic to cats that he sneezed and swelled all the way through *The Lion King*. Beverly is allergic to my leaving dirty socks on the floor. Meredith is allergic to her brother. In my research, I discovered that some people are allergic to cockroaches. They are especially sensitive if, as one source stated, "the cockroach droppings become airborne." Don't we have enough to worry about? Will that become part of our weather forecast and pollen report? "Our forecast for tomorrow is partly cloudy skies, 30 percent chance of rain, and the pollen level will be high with a 75 percent chance of being hit with airborne cockroach droppings."

The best way to deal with allergies is to be informed, and there are some complicated terms involved. For example, *antihistamines* are bombs placed around your yard to blow up any antihistas that get too close; *spores* are made with graham crackers, chocolate, and marshmallows, and are placed in the oven at 300 degrees; and *rhinitis* is an inflammation in the skin that causes your driver's license picture to resemble an African rhino.

Parasites are two sites walking together; *pet allergens* are allergens that are housebroken; and *hypersensitivity* is a condition you discover your wife has when you ask her, "Honey, you're not really going to buy those shoes, are you?" For relief, we must ask ourselves a very disturbing but necessary question: "Do we really want to take a drug called *St. John's Wort?*" Allergies are a real pain, but relief comes with the right medication.

It is a similar problem for people who suffer from spiritual allergies. They may be allergic to things like love, kindness, and grace. A child, a friend, an employee, a minister, or a church member fails to perform to *our* level of expectation. We react, not by coughing, sneezing, and wheezing but by griping, gossiping, and whining—wonderful words of strife.

We will continue to suffer from spiritual allergies as long as we respond to people out of legalism instead of grace. There is a remedy for spiritual allergies, but we must ask ourselves a sometimes disturbing question: "Do we really want relief?" If we are serious, it is right under our noses in something called *St. John's Word:* "I command you to love each other in the same way that I love you" (John 15:12 NLT).

Spiritual allergies, unlike physical ones, originate in the heart. Relief comes when we apply the right meditation.

The Silence in Your Voice Leaves a Very Loud Echo

It is obvious after talking to some people that they do not understand how important words are to the English language. It is impossible to communicate without them . . . unless you are listening to rap music or a political campaign speech, or trying to buy milk at a convenience store in New York City. Without words, there would be no blank expressions on the faces of my dogs when I try to carry on a normal conversation with them. They look at me like I have horns. Without words, we would have no spel chek on our computers, really short sermons, and no way to communicate with church basketball referees except through gestures.

Words make it possible for fairy-tale income-tax reports and hallway politics at Baptist meetings. If there were no words, teenagers would not be able to plead, "But everyone else will be there!" The biggest drawback to having a wordless society would be that we could no longer irritate our high-school English teacher by misusing participles or ending a sentence with a presbyterian.

Communication through words has been the focus of some famous quotes throughout history. From the Revolutionary War, we all remember John Paul Jones Stewart's wife, Martha, who said, "I have not yet begun to fight"; Israel Putnam at the Battle of Enron Hill, with his classic quote, "Don't file till you see the whites of their lies"; and Thomas Inalotta Paine, who invented the first coin-operated restroom. He wrote about his invention in a famous pamphlet, *Common Cents,* and said, "These are the dimes that dry men's soles."

From World War II, we have Glenn Miller MacArthur, a trombone player in the Philippines, who proclaimed after a concert fiasco, "I shall retune!" One of the more memorable quotes comes from the pen of the greatest televangepoet of the twentieth century, Ernie Frost, who wrote, "The wallets are lovely, marked, and deep. But I have creditors to meet, and aisles to go before I sleep, and aisles to go before I sleep."

If we were to be honest with one another, we might see that many of us as brothers, sisters, sons, daughters, fathers, or mothers may be remembered more for what we didn't say than what we did say. Did you ever hear the words "I love you" when you were a child? Do you ever say it to your children? Do you ever say it to your spouse? In your conversations, do words of praise flow as freely as words of criticism? Or worse, do you pass on every opportunity for encouragement and simply say nothing at all? Too often when friends and loved ones need our comforting, encouraging, or congratulatory words the most, all they get is silence.

What we do not say in those situations speaks volumes about ourselves. Silence may be golden . . . but seldom does it have a silver lining.

Actions Do Speak Louder Than Words, Except for Car Stereos

Peoeple are always coming up with creative ways to make a statement without words. In the '60s, it was either a peace sign or long hair, toward neither of which did I have an inclination. Preschoolers throw a tantrum (which a good parent will always throw back); children stamp their feet, turn the corners of their mouths down, and storm out of the room; and teenagers make statements by the clothes they almost wear.

Adult women have mastered a glare that could melt a heat-seeking missile and the art of spontaneously erupting into uncontrollable crying. Neither one is a pretty sight, and the adult male has no option but to tuck his tail between his legs and run. Teenagers also make statements without words with the abuse of a car stereo. In the trunk of my son's car is an amplifier big enough to sleep a family of four, if they had industrial-strength earplugs. If I stand on my deck, I can hear him driving through Kentucky.

It goes something like this: I will be on my front porch at three in the morning waiting for David to come home. Off in the distance, in Kentucky, there is a pulsating, *Close Encounters of the Third Kind*-like rumbling, accompanied by the slow-but-gaining-in-intensity vibration of all my inner organs. My first inclination is to look upward, expecting a Klingon wessel ("vessel" to you people who don't speak like Chekov) to land on my face. Then I think maybe he traded his Mustang for a shuttle launch. You can buy almost anything on the Internet.

As I think of a third alternative, I remember his ohminous words, "It has 80 watts per channel, minimum RMS @ 25 ohms, from 65 Hz to 12 kHz, with no more than 1 percent total harmonic distortion." To which I replied, "Huh?" It was one of those special communication moments in a father-son relationship. But he is making a statement. He is saying he doesn't care if he damages my eardrums. I SAID, *HE DOESN'T CARE IF HE'S DAMAGING MY EARDRUMS!*

Teenagers rank right up there with wives when it comes to making statements without words. They pale in comparison to Jesus. Whether it was turning water into wine, walking on water, or washing the disciples' feet, Jesus wrote the book on it. Oh, don't get me wrong. He spoke the greatest words ever spoken, but I'm afraid we too often ignore the significance of His actions.

Jesus's favorite phrase to describe Himself was "Son of Man," a term of servanthood—a term of action, not words. He listened, He loved, He served. As Christians, we would do well to follow that pattern. Our children, friends, and neighbors are waiting for us to make a statement, but they probably quit listening to our words a long time ago. Our best opportunity to make a statement for Jesus is to give our tongues a rest . . . and exercise our hands, our feet, and our hearts.

Chapter 10:
Joy to the World the Lord Is Calm

Lessons from the Holidays

I Know You've Been Dazed, but Have You Been Holidazed?

I have a bone to pick with our founding fathers. They put a major holiday in every month except August. We have to go from the Fourth of July to Labor Day without a good reason for furniture sales. The best we can come up with is "Back to School Daze," and what teacher in her right mind wants to celebrate that?

January has New Year's Day and Martin Luther King Jr. Day; February has Valentine's Day, Presidents' Day, and Super Bowl Sunday; March has St. Patrick's Day and sometimes Good Friday/ Easter; April has April Fools' Day, sometimes Good Friday/Easter, Administrative Professionals Day, and the NBA playoffs.

May has Mother's Day, Memorial Day, and the NBA playoffs; June has Flag Day, Father's Day, and the NBA playoffs; July has Independence Day; September has Labor Day; October has Columbus Day and Halloween; November has Veterans Day and the Detroit Lions Playing Football on Thanksgiving Day Day; and December has long lines and short tempers.

There are a few minor unofficial holidays on the calendar during this eight-week stretch in summer that most people do not celebrate. July is Read an Almanac Month and Anti-Boredom Month. Don't they cancel each other out? July is National Baked Beans Month, but August 23 is Ride the Wind Day. July 5 is Workaholics Day. Of course, there is no day off for this. July 13 is Fools' Paradise Day. This is mostly celebrated in Southern California. In Alabama it is sometimes celebrated on July 20, which is Ugly Truck Contest Day.

July 14 is National Nude Day. This should probably be celebrated on July 11, which is National Cheer Up the Lonely Day. August 8 is National Senior Citizens Day, which should never be combined with National Nude Day. August is Romance Awareness Month. I was not aware of that. August is also National Catfish Month and National Golf Month. This means men can celebrate Romance Awareness Month by taking their wives fishing or playing golf with them.

We spend a lot of time, money, and energy anticipating and ultimately celebrating the major holidays. Sometimes the stress and pressure of the holidays, especially Thanksgiving and Christmas, has us in such a frenzy that we spend most of these seasons in a mind-numbing daze, usually leaving us in no condition to celebrate. We let the holidays get to us. We become holidazed.

Why do we let that happen? Then again, why are we only thankful in November? Why are we only giving in December? Why can't we do things for other people for no reason at all, just because it's the right thing to do? We don't have to have a holiday to celebrate life.

Why can't we make "holidazed" a positive term? Has someone done something nice for you for no apparent reason? You've been holidazed. In the words of Jesus and Clint Eastwood . . . go and do likewise. Holidaze someone. Go ahead. It will make their day.

Does the Cock Still Crow?

History is full of important history . . . especially historical history-making decisions. One of the most historical and history-inducing events in the life of our young spunky country was the Revolutionary War, sometimes called the War for American Independence, or the First War of Typographical Errors, the first being the *singing* of the Declaration of Independence.

An important event leading up to the war was another typographical error in a nasty memo from the British government threatening a tax. Because of the embarrassing error, we seldom read in history books about the significance of the Boston Pea Party. The colonists received a revised memo and did the tea thing in Boston Harbor.

Several years later, Thomas Jefferson was elected president because voters erroneously reasoned that if he could write the Declaration of Independence, he could explain the electoral college.

Actually, he was elected because of yet another typographical error. The voters got disgusted with what they thought were the Alien and Sedation Acts. They thought these were a series of laws passed by John Adams that gave aliens free dental work. It was not until Jefferson was elected that they realized it was supposed to be Alien and Sedition Acts, a harmless policy that gave aliens free seditions.

Jefferson then made a decision that would change the United States forever. He outlawed funny pants and gaudy wigs. This law stood until the 1970s. However, his big decision was to buy New Orleans and the Louisiana Territory. Once he experienced Mardi Gras, cayenne pepper, and crawdads, he tried to give New Orleans back.

Our forefathers had a lot of decisions to make. Their choices laid the groundwork for a new and expanding country. They chose freedom over tyranny. It sounds sort of biblical. A lot of decisions were made before, during, and after the crucifixion of Christ. There were no typographical errors. The people knew exactly what they were doing. Pilate chose not to decide. The crowd chose Barabbas instead of Jesus. The Jewish leaders chose law rather than faith. Jesus chose God rather than self. Judas chose money instead of the Master. Peter chose denial rather than commitment.

Easter reminds us of a decision we have to make in life. What will we do with Jesus? It is not just a one-time choice. We have to choose daily to follow Jesus. We deny Christ whenever we choose anger over gentleness, hate instead of love, arrogance over humility, or sour grapes instead of the fruit of the Spirit. Easter reminds us to look at Jesus and answer the question. Yes, the cock still crows . . . and people still cry, "Give us Barabbas!"

Which Came First: the Freedom or the Grave?

He is a forgotten man. He was born in St. Clairsville, Ohio. If you travel to the town of Nettuno, Italy, east of Anzio and about twenty miles outside of Rome, you will find an American Battle Monument Cemetery. One of the dead buried there is Sylvester Antolak, Sergeant, U.S. Army, 15th Infantry, 3rd Division. On May 24, 1944, Sergeant Antolak was out in front of his squad when they ran into a German position. As he led the attack on the position, he was wounded three times and knocked to the ground but continued his advance. He was killed after helping to clear the way for his company to advance.

He is a forgotten man. He was born in Byesville, Ohio. If you travel to Byesville today, about eighty miles east of Columbus, you will find Greenwood Cemetery. One of the dead buried there is Herbert F. Christian, Private, U.S. Army, 15th Infantry, 3rd Division. On June 2, 1944, Private Christian was in a scout unit that was ambushed by sixty German riflemen, three machine guns, and three tanks. Private Christian took it upon himself to charge the enemy and try to cover the retreat of his twelve comrades. He killed several enemy soldiers, allowing the rest of his unit to escape. He died during the action.

He, too, is a forgotten man. He was born in Bivalve, New Jersey. If you visit Boston, Massachusetts, and travel south along the coast for twenty miles, you will enter the small town of Scituate. Go to Union Cemetery and you will find the grave of Elden H. Johnson, Private, U.S. Army, 15th Infantry, 3rd Division. On June 2, 1944, Private Johnson was with Private Christian in their battle near Valmontine, Italy. He also tried to distract the enemy long enough for the rest of the unit to retreat. Private Johnson killed five enemy soldiers and destroyed one of the machine-gun nests before he was killed by machine-gun fire.

These soldiers have several things in common. They were all killed in action. They were all awarded the Congressional Medal of Honor, posthumously, for that action. They have one other thing in common. They all served in the 3rd Division. They are forgotten heroes, but you have heard of one of their comrades. His name was Audie Murphy. Sergeant Antolak was even in the same Company as Murphy.

Sylvester Antolak, Herbert Christian, and Elden Johnson never experienced a welcome-home parade. The last image they had of this great country was from a troopship headed out of the harbor on what turned out to be a one-way trip to a foreign land. They died too young. War does that.

That is why we have Memorial Day. It reminds us of the sacrifices of forgotten heroes. It gives us the chance to be grateful. At least for a few minutes on one day of the year, we can honor the memories of those who gave their lives for our freedom. Memorial Day is a reminder that we will always be the land of the free . . . and the home of the grave.

*Our Fodder, Who Art in Heaven,
Halloween Be My Name*

all is officially here, and that means it's time for cool weather,
pumpkins, and Halloween. In the same sense as your third
cousin who still wears plaid pants, pumpkins are a fruit. They
are from the Gourd family. The proud parents were Rufus and
Ervina Gourd of Gourdonsville, Tennessee. Ervina was a home-
maker and Rufus was a military man, having served for a while
in the Tennessee National Gourd. The largest pumpkin on record
was more than thirteen hundred pounds. Mrs. Gourd was in labor
for two years.

Pumpkins have three main purposes in life. Give one to your
grandmother and make her bake you a pumpkin pie at Thanksgiving. Take several of them when they are overripe and smash
them in your neighbor's yard, but don't let your parents find out.
Take a large pumpkin and hollow it out. With one of your rela-

tives as a guide, carve an ugly face in it. Then fill it with green Jell-O and watch it ooze out over time. It's fun, in a Stephen King sort of way.

In a seemingly unrelated story, a man in England was busy toasting some crumpets. When he pulled out one batch, he discovered one that looked like Jesus. This of course would be from that great old English hymn, "When the crumpet of the Lord shall sound and time shall be no more . . ." The man decided not to cash in on his fame. He just took it to a nearby pub and displayed it to his astounded friends. You would think people in pubs would be accustomed to seeing Jesus in a crumpet.

In another seemingly unrelated story, South Korea has decided to beautify its beaches. That sounds nice and routine, doesn't it? If you guessed trash pickup, cleaning, and seaweed removal you would be normal, but you would be wrong. They are going to remove all of the barbed wire from the beaches. I can just picture conversations in Asia between husbands and wives. "Honey, you want to go to South Korea this summer for a vacation? They've removed all the barbed wire from the beaches." "Well, OK, as long as they leave the land mines and unexploded bombs."

Why are people so quick to find Jesus in a piece of toast, a burrito, a crumpet, a cloud, or a pile of mashed potatoes? Those same people see Christians every day. Why do we never hear them say, after they've seen one of us, "I've just seen Jesus"? Why is it easier to see Jesus in a piece of toast than it is in us? Could it be that we are wearing a mask and Jesus is always covered up? The Bible says, "You were . . . created to be like God, truly righteous and holy" (Ephesians 4:24 GW).

Inauthentic Christians become fodder for those who like to fire shots at anything holy. People cannot see Jesus in us until we remove our masks. It's easy to remove the barbed wire and beautify our appearance. We can attend church and sing religious songs. We have to spend more time on the land mines of anger and resentment and the unexploded bombs of depression and self-doubt.

It is Halloween. Halloween masks are temporary. Is yours?

The Color of Freedom

The time was autumn of 1944. The place was the Vosges Mountains of eastern France. Two hundred seventy-five men of the 1st Battalion, 141st Infantry, had been cut off for six days behind the German lines. They were running out of food, water, and ammunition. But they were rescued by men of the 442nd Regimental Combat Team, the most decorated regiment in the war—with one Medal of Honor, fifty-two Distinguished Service Crosses, 569 Silver Stars, and over 800 Bronze Stars. One other interesting fact about the 442nd. They were Japanese-Americans.

The time was August 6, 1950, in an assembly area north of Pusan, in the mountains of North Korea. It was a little-known place in an unfortunately forgotten war. Private William Thompson was a machine gunner in the 24th Regiment when his unit was attacked. While Thompson covered them during their retreat, he was wounded but kept firing until his men dragged him away. He broke free and crawled back to his machine gun. His men survived. He did not. William Thompson was an African-American.

The time was May 2, 1968. It was a place called Loc Ninh, a Green Beret outpost near the Cambodian border. It was a little-known place in an unpopular war. A cry for help came over the radio from a twelve-man team surrounded in the jungle. Just before a three-man helicopter crew took off on a rescue operation, a thirty-two-year-old sergeant jumped on board. When they reached the squad, the sergeant leaped out of the helicopter and began carrying dead and wounded. During the next six hours, he was wounded several times but still managed to call in for more help and get the wounded out. His own wounds were so severe he was given up for dead and placed in a body bag. He survived and won the Medal of Honor. His name was Roy Benevidez. He was a Mexican-American.

Like the locations of the battles, veterans come in all shapes, sizes, and colors. They formed a bond only found in combat. The veterans of World War II fought for each other and a cause . . . and it changed the world. The veterans of Korea and Vietnam fought for the one standing next to them in the trench or walking beside them in the jungle, changing them forever. There was no color, no race, no social standing. There was a brotherhood.

It is Veterans Day. It is celebrated in cities and towns all over the United States. Ignore what you may see in television advertising or newspaper sales circulars. This day is not about shopping. It is about honoring those who served. It is a time of remembering and appreciating. They were ordinary men and women, forced into unimaginable circumstances, who deserve our extraordinary thanks.

The color of freedom is never black, white, brown, or yellow. It is always red, from the blood of the veterans who shed it.

The Hit and Myth of Thanksgiving

T hanksgiving Day will see the largest gathering of turkeys of the year, except for the annual meeting of the people who plan the fall television season. To fully understand the history of Thanksgiving we must go back to 1620, when the Pilgrims left England for a place free of Wal-Mart SuperCenters. On the voyage over, the Pilgrims called themselves the "Saints," while the others were referred to as "Strangers." These later evolved into "Baptists" and "Methodists."

They brought with them three important celebrations: the Sabbath, a Day of Thanksgiving, and a Day of Humiliation. Baptists later expanded the Day of Humiliation into Clergy Appreciation Month. Another major contribution was the cornucopia, which actually originated in ancient Greece. When the ancient Greeks would take off their sandals, their ancient wives would scream, "Put those sandals back on your feet! You've got a cornucopia!"

As with any holiday, there are certain myths that surround Thanksgiving. The biggest myth concerns the meal at the first Thanksgiving. Historians only agree there was a staple of fowl and venison, probably killed with staple guns. The meat was roasted by several people turning the spit . . . which is the same phrase used to describe wedding vows in some rural areas of the Oklahoma panhandle.

The Pilgrims had no forks. They ate with spoons, knives, and their fingers. This is still the most preferred method of dining by college football players. The most frustrating myth is that the Pilgrims always wore black and white. This is wrong. The only time they wore black and white was when they were under attack by Indians from the air. The Pilgrims would lie down next to each other and disguise themselves as a giant piano. Many of these Pilgrims grew tired of diving on the ground and looking like a piano and moved south, where we get the term . . . Florida Keys.

There are still myths surrounding Thanksgiving. For the Christian, it is not a holiday to be celebrated on one day but a holy idea to be continued throughout the year. We need to carry the idea of thanksgiving with us all the time, because we have much for which to be thankful. Living in America, we have become spoiled and take everything for granted. There are times we don't even attend church with a heart and attitude of thanksgiving.

Psalm 100 is subtitled, "A Psalm of Thanksgiving." It contains the lines, "Worship the LORD with gladness . . . enter his gates with thanksgiving . . . give thanks to him . . . his steadfast love endures forever" (vv. 2, 4, 5 NRSV). That's why we celebrate.

Is Thanksgiving a myth to you? It is if you only think about it one day a year. Go ahead and celebrate Thanksgiving this week, but live your life every day with an attitude of thankfulness. Don't myth out on Thanksgiving.

lesson 97

O Come, All Ye Faithless, Joyless, and Unyielding

Even to the untrained eye, there are many clues that Christmas is almost here. The movie *It's a Wonderful Life* plays twelve times a day. During the holidays, there will be 731 college football games on television. Families are making detailed plans to celebrate the most blessed event of the year . . . the wrestling match that takes place after deciding which in-laws to go to on what day and discussing which grandparents will become the most belligerent when they get the news.

Children are whining about toys, and the last remains of Thanksgiving dinner have escaped from the refrigerator and are soon to become the subject of an Anne Rice novel. It's the most wonderful time of the year. But the ultimate warning of an incoming Christmas is mail-order gift catalogs offering everything from a book entitled *U.S. Government Benefits* (Isn't that an oxymoron?) to an insect wall clock that advertises "a different insect

sound every hour." I don't want to hear insect sounds every hour. That's why I don't spend much time in my basement.

Through the years, many of you have said this to your spouse but did nothing: "We ought to get each of our ministers a Christmas present this year." Well, maybe this is the year. How about a dance video? One guarantees I will become a "hot nightclub and party dancer." I don't get a lot of requests to dance, but I need it. Watching me dance is like watching worms melt.

Or I might like a motion-activated plastic guard dog. It responds with loud barking if anything moves past its plastic electronic eye. That would be great, if I am ever robbed by plastic burglars. There is a mystery electronic top that "spins for days with no apparent explanation." Meredith did the same thing when she was a cheerleader. The most popular gift is a portable fog device. It must be popular, because I see a lot of people who seem to carry fog with them wherever they go.

I will be the first to admit that Christmas is my favorite time of the year, including giving and receiving gifts. Most of the gifts I am given are meant for me. I don't have to share them. The greatest gift I was ever given was Jesus. I have to share Him, but how? Witnessing is one way. But sharing the Gift is more than that. It is living a life so full of joy it overflows to the people we see every day.

Joy has come into the world in the form of a baby. We should be the most joyous people in the world. Sometimes I wonder where the joy has gone. What some people share is not joy, and it is definitely not the Jesus I know. If we don't know the joy of Christmas, we'd better find it. Come to the manger . . . the faithful, the joyful, and the triumphant will meet you there.

Lesson 98

Just Dreaming of a Yearlong Christmas . . . Color Is Optional

I had a dream the other night. This was not one of my normal dreams like Elvis being abducted by Jimmy Hoffa. This dream was odd. I was the leader of a religious cult called Servants of the American Dream (S.A.D.), who only met during the Xmas season. We were a small, conservative group and held services in the Ralph Lauren section of Saks Fifth Avenue.

For our Confessional Greed, we believed: (1) in the unquestionable and complete authority of the *Wall Street Journal*, regardless of the typesetting; (2) in no alien immersion, unless the aliens landed in Nebraska wearing leisure suits; (3) in the Father, the Son, and the Holy Esprit. Each day at noon, during December, we stopped whatever we were doing and placed twenty-dollar bills on our foreheads. We then bowed down and offered a one-minute prayer to the nearest bank. A group of liberals once stirred up a controversy by asking to pray to a branch bank because of the convenience. We dealt with them by locking them inside Kmart the day after Thanksgiving during a blue-light special. They have caused no trouble since.

Each year on Xmas Eve, we had a big "Xmas with the Stars, but Not with the Poor and Needy" celebration at the Hollywood Bowl. We sang our favorite carols: "Away in a Merger," "While Shepherds Discounted Their Flocks," and "I Heard the Sales on Christmas Day," and then listened to some Hollywood personality give his testi*money* about what Xmas means to him.

The climax of the evening came when our guest speaker, Slug Slugmun, presented his famous inspirational message based on three historically popular holiday themes: The Role of Women in Xmas Shopping, Is Kermit the Frog the Earth Beast Referred to in the Thirteenth Chapter of Revelation?, and Is Frosty the Snowman the Antichrist? For research on Revelation and Frosty the Snowman, Slugmun consulted every existing authority known to man, including Marvel Comics, Dr. Seuss, and Gene Autry.

To the person in the crowd who had spent the most Sundays Xmas shopping, we were about to give a copy of Reader's Digest's new book, *How to Condense the Xmas Story,* when I woke up from my dream.

I tried, but I couldn't go back to sleep. I kept thinking about another *Christ*mas story. This story also included shopping for presents but the people had a different attitude. They were patient, kind, loving, and forgiving, and they were like that all during the year.

This *Christ*mas story was also different in another way. It had an unusual beginning, in a manger of all places. The people attending were not big-name personalities, but lowly shepherds. This *Christ*mas story had no fanfare. It began with "The Word became flesh and dwelt among us." But it didn't end there. It began again with "Why do you seek the living among the dead? He is not here. He is risen."

Merry Xmas or Merry *Christ*mas? You have to decide.

There Is a Calm in Gilead

During the holidays, my family carried on a tradition begun hundreds of years ago when the Pilgrims celebrated that first Christmas in America by shopping for socks, cologne, and a cheese log for that certain loved one. Christmas hasn't been the same since. We went Christmas shopping at the mall. It was like watching an ant farm after filling it with espresso. At least it was like that for the females. They scurried back and forth carrying packages weighing ten times their own body weight while the males just lounged in the nests they had made in the comfortable chairs scattered throughout the mall colony, wishing they were at home giving themselves an appendectomy.

Shopping at the mall may not be actual chaos, but it is a rude cousin. To fully appreciate the mall, sing the following lines to the tune of "Deck the Halls": "Deck the mall with lots of people, shopping for a gift I know not what; Standing here amid the elbows, I will be in line until I rot."

CHAPTER 10: Joy to the World, the Lord Is Calm

Why do we put up with the chaos of the mall, which always includes singing frogs, dancing fish, barking dogs, and belching Santas? (Or was that at my brother's house?) We do it so we can experience Christmas morning. Most people probably have a Christmas-morning ritual that has all the grace and charm of a society tea party. At our house, it's more like a rugby scrum. Empty, torn boxes are everywhere while surprised and somewhat perturbed Chihuahuas lay whimpering in the corner, wounded by projectile wads of wrapping paper.

Hershey, our once-proud Yorkshire terrier, is cowering on the sofa, embarrassed because he is covered in red and green bows. There is a trail of destruction in the house surpassed only by Sherman's march through Georgia. (Historical side note—years later, after the college football bowl games, it was proven it would have been much easier for Sherman to march through Alabama, Mississippi, or South Carolina.)

No matter how chaotic it may get in the mall, we always seem to find the object(s) of our search. It was like that at the first Christmas. Amid the chaos of Herod's rule, the magi of long ago found the object of their search, and they found it in the peaceful setting of a stable. That was only the beginning. Jesus was the Captain of calm, the Prince of peace.

For the disciples on the Sea of Galilee, Jesus was the calm in the midst of a raging storm. In the chaotic days of Lazarus's death, Jesus calmed Mary and Martha. During the chaos of the Cross, we find Jesus calmly asking God to forgive those around Him.

We all face difficult times. In the midst of the chaos surrounding those events we sometimes lose sight of Christ, but the Christ of Christmas never loses sight of us. Bethlehem's reach will always go just beyond where we are. Joy to the world . . . the Lord is calm.

*Donder and Blitzen Caught
Cheating in Reindeer Games*

I learned in a college journalism course that many people only read articles in the newspaper with attention-grabbing head-lines. For example, "Oregon Woman Dressed in Abraham Lincoln Costume Pilots Single-Engine Plane over New Mexico, Gives Birth to Alien" would immediately get my attention. One of the more infamous headlines appeared in the Chicago *Daily Tribune* in November 1948. It read, "Dewey Defeats Truman!" (For those of you who are presidentially impaired, Truman actually defeated Dewey.)

The very next day, Truman went deer hunting and spoke those forever immortal and misquoted words, "The buck dropped here!" If you remember your history, you will recall that on one of his campaign trips he got so mad during a speech aimed at the Russians he said he would call down a storm from the clouds. In a spontaneous moment of patriotic excitement one of his aides yelled, "Give 'em hail, Harry!"

Without a doubt, though, the greatest place in the world for catching interesting headlines is the checkout line at the supermarket. Once I have finished counting the items in the baskets of people who are in the "Ten Items or Less" line, I like to look at the tabloids. They read something like this: "Farmer in Idaho Grows Potato That Looks Like Richard Nixon" (I thought all potatoes looked like Richard Nixon). Others could be: "Aliens Land in California—Two Elected to Congress," "Elvis Seen Ballooning in Nevada—Mistaken for Goodyear Blimp," "Trucker in Alabama Truck Stop Sees the Face of Moses in His Chicken Fried Steak" (How would he know what Moses looked like?), and "Man Lands on Mars—Luggage Goes to Cleveland."

Man has always been fascinated by bizarre stories. They sell papers. Two thousand years ago an event happened, so spectacular that it would have appeared like this in the Bethlehem tabloid: "Virgin Gives Birth to Savior of the World in a Stable." I can hear the laughter now . . . except this time, the headline would have been true. The way of the manger *is* spectacular and yet simple at the same time. Spectacular because of the circumstances, simple because of the surroundings.

That whole manger scenario always has been, and always will be, eternally connected to the Cross event—the opening act of a world-changing play. And yet the simple story of the manger, when understood at its deepest level, is the essence of Christmas. Jesus could not stay in the inn . . . and ultimately, neither could He stay in the tomb. Merry Christmas.